SINGERS OF TODAY

Victoria de los Angeles

PLATE I

SINGERS
OF TODAY

by

DONALD BROOK

SALISBURY SQUARE · LONDON

First published 1949
Second impression 1950
Second (Revised) Edition 1958

©

BY DONALD BROOK
1958

Made and Printed in Great Britain by
CHARLES BIRCHALL & SONS LTD
James Street, Liverpool, 1

CONTENTS

5

ILLUSTRATIONS

ILLUSTRATIONS

INTRODUCTORY NOTE

THIS collection of sketches of prominent singers does not, of course, pretend to be comprehensive, for in England alone there are more vocalists of some standing than could possibly be accommodated in a single volume. The absence of any particular artist, therefore, does not mean that I am unappreciative of his or her merits.

It will also be observed that I have not confined my selection entirely to singers who are either "blooming" or "booming" at the present time. I have included several of the older singers who now devote most of their time to the art of teaching because I feel sure the reader would agree that they have something significant to contribute to a volume of this nature.

The reader will also understand that as I have encouraged my "sitters" to express their opinions freely, the ideas and advice of some must inevitably conflict with the views and recommendations of others.

Finally, mention of any particular recording does not necessarily mean that it is a good one. One very often discovers a good performance marred by bad recording, or a mediocre performance made tolerable by sympathetic recording, and one can only advise the reader to hear a record right through before buying it.

DONALD BROOK

Revised Edition,
March, 1958.

Norman Allin

I T seems to be generally agreed that in music the artist who "looks the part" possesses some slight advantage over those whose personal appearance suggests that they follow a less attractive calling. In other words, we should all be a trifle disappointed if we went to the opera and found a prima donna closely resembling the vinegary spinster who had just snapped at us from behind the counter of the local post-office.

Norman Allin has this advantage. As soon as you see him you think: "Here is a man with a bottom D". He is the typical Big Bass: tall and well-built, genial and full of honest north-country humour and commonsense, kind and generous. Nation-wide recognition of his great gifts, of his varied experience, has had no effect upon his modesty: he is still the sincere, homely soul he has always been.

He was born in the Lancashire town of Ashton-under-Lyne, son of a printer and publisher who spent much of his spare time in amateur music-making, but removed at a very early age to the village of New Hey, near Rochdale. There was nothing of the pampered prodigy about his childhood: he went to the village school, which was run by his uncle, and distinguished himself not in music but at cricket. He learned the game on a cinder path.

When the time came for him to decide what he wanted to do in the world he disappointed his father by showing no great inclination to go into the printing trade. Architecture was the subject that appealed most strongly to him, and with a somewhat vague idea about working up from the bottom, he went into the building trade as an apprentice, for his people were not in a position to article him to an architect in the usual way.

In those early days, music was just a delightful hobby. He had sung in the choir of the local Methodist chapel as a boy, and was wondering how his voice was going to settle down after the inevitable breaking process. Only a very limited time could now be devoted to it: he used to rise well before five o'clock in the morning, do a hard day's work, then go off to evening classes at Rochdale

Technical School to study mathematics and architecture. He usually got back home at about nine-thirty, and was in bed soon after ten.

His fine bass voice developed quickly, and he was doing solo work at the age of seventeen. At about this time he began to realize that his voice might possibly open the door to the musical profession. Even so, he started to study harmony with a local teacher and to dream of becoming not a singer but a cathedral organist! But Norman Allin was never a 'dreamer' in the popular sense: he was far too practical a young man. His voice was his greatest musical asset, so he put it to the best possible use. Some idea of his thoroughness may be gained from the fact that in order to sing lieder intelligently he went off to additional evening classes to study German.

Opportunity generally comes at least once to every enterprising young man. It presented itself to Norman Allin when he was twenty in the shape of a scholarship to the Royal Manchester College of Music, and was seized forthwith.

So the embryo architect became a music student. Everybody thought he would concentrate upon singing, and a little disappointment was expressed when during his four years at that northern college he did not win a single prize for the vocal art! Nobody imagined for one moment that he would ever become a famous singer.

The explanation, of course, is that Norman Allin was not worrying about singing: he had made up his mind to become a Doctor of Music and was devoting the greater part of his time to theoretical subjects. There is not the slightest doubt that he would have attained his object had circumstances not forced him once again to make use of his greatest musical gift. His four-year scholarship at £60 a year was now running out, and financial problems were looming up ahead. At that time, too, he was thinking a lot about a beautiful young lady named Edith Clegg. He had known her since childhood and from the age of twelve had been thrilled merely to see her walk down the street. Even if that distant doctorate were achieved, it would be many years before he could earn sufficient to ask her to marry him. A substantial sum of money had to be earned and saved fairly quickly, and that could not be done by giving half-crown music lessons. So his voice had to solve the problem.

His first singing engagements were at the local chapels: he can still remember those Pleasant Sunday Afternoons, as they were

NORMAN ALLIN

called, at which he sang for five shillings a time! However, even these humble affairs helped to establish him as a singer. Bookings for the *Messiah* or for concerts at a guinea apiece began to come in so frequently that he was encouraged to raise his fees, more people came to him for lessons, and with this encouragement, Norman Allin and Edith Clegg, who was then a schoolteacher, became engaged. They were married in 1912.

A year later, Norman Allin came to London, as thousands of other enterprising northerners have done, in search of fortune. The late Sir Henry J. Wood, who was always a kind friend to gifted and sincere young artists, heard him sing and wrote on his behalf to the organizers of the Norwich Triennial Festival urging them to engage him for the 1914 Festival. Fame, it seemed, was now just round the corner, but a bitter disappointment was in store for him: the Great War broke out and the Festival was cancelled.

With very mixed feelings, Allin went to the barracks at Bury to offer his services, but to his surprise he was classified in a low medical grade and was sent home to await call-up. It was rather a disappointment, but he was relieved to know that for the present at least, his career would not be interrupted.

The next milestone in his life story is the occasion upon which he sang to Sir Thomas Beecham. The famous conductor was so impressed with his treatment of arias from *Die Walküre*, *The Magic Flute* and *Boris Godunof* that, somewhat rashly, he offered Allin the title rôle of *Boris Godunof*. The young singer stood aghast. How could he, with little or no experience in opera, take such an important part? It was a great temptation, but Allin decided that it would be foolish to attempt it without a lengthy period of coaching and some sort of stage experience in minor parts. Beecham agreed that it would probably be better to start in a small way, and accordingly offered him the part of the Old Hebrew in *Samson and Delilah*. It was a happy choice. Nobody could have played the part better, and Beecham showed his appreciation by offering him several more important rôles during the next six months. He played Boris some years later at Covent Garden, and was a tremendous success.

Meanwhile, in oratorio and general concert work he was making just as rapid strides, and throughout the nineteen-twenties the choral societies of Great Britain were persistent in their demands for his services as a soloist. One can well understand that some of the more popular oratorios became wearisome to him, and it is not surprising to note that after he had given his 270th performance of the *Messiah* at a Hallé concert in 1932 he declared that he would not sing in it again. He has kept his vow.

Norman Allin has never been very fond of travelling—at least, not of the sort of endless travelling that most musical virtuosi have to endure—but he has very happy memories of the visit he made to Australia in 1934 when he took part in an opera season lasting over seven months at Melbourne and Sydney. At Colombo, on his return journey, he received a cable asking if he would accept a professorship at the Royal Academy of Music. He felt he could not refuse this honour, and accordingly took up his duties there in the autumn of 1935. A few years later he was given a similar appointment at the Royal Manchester College of Music, and he held this as well until 1942, when pressure of work made it impossible for him to travel north every week.

It is scarcely necessary to say much about Norman Allin's fine resonant voice: there must be few music lovers in this country who have not heard and admired it. His compass is nearly two-and-a half octaves (F down to bottom C) and even his high notes—which are generally a source of trouble to deep basses over middle age—are perfectly controlled.

He believes that to be a proper bass, a man needs a range of two octaves at least: D to D, and by this he does not mean an *occasional* bottom D! Only in a very few cases can a young baritone be developed into a bass, because as a rule, a voice can be trained upwards to some extent, but rarely downwards. If, however, the notes are there, a great deal can be done to increase the weight of them by proper development, but that is an art that cannot be discussed briefly.

Norman Allin does not pretend to have any secret or wonderful "method" of teaching, and is dubious about many of the "theories" put forward in modern times. Give him a promising voice to train and he will make a good job of it, provided, of course, that its owner is willing to work. It is significant that he never speaks to his pupils about vocal registers: the singer should not be conscious of them.

He enjoys teaching but the novice is apt to be bewildered by his candour. On approaching him for an audition one cannot fail to notice a businesslike air mingled with his geniality. He will probably say: "Do you mind if I tell you frankly if you're no good?" If one gets through the ordeal satisfactorily one can proceed to pull his leg a trifle, which is well worth while if only to witness the sly little smile that he reserves for such occasions.

His chief complaint about the rising generation of singers is that they generally want to "arrive" too quickly: they should become good musicans as well as good singers before they demand big fees. Among these young singers there are some fine voices which, if properly developed, will be as good as anything we have heard in the past fifty years or so, but Norman Allin is feeling some concern about the lack of personality in so many of the students of today. He doubts whether any of them will grow up into such fine characters as those remarkable singers of yesterday: Robert Radford, John Coates, Gervase Elwes and Frank Mullings.

He is interested in the work of our contemporary British composers, believing that they are the equals of the composers of any other nation in the world today. He particularly admires William Walton, and is fascinated by the remarkable originality of the operas of Benjamin Britten, although he feels it is too early to pass judgement upon them: they still have to prove themselves by holding their place in the repertoires of the opera companies.

Whenever he gets tired of the bustle of life in London, Allin likes to escape to the Cotswold hills and there to spend two or three days in walking alone. This beautiful part of England has always been a great inspiration to him and he never tires of those gracious hills and valleys with their pleasing stone-built farm-houses and cottages. When he cannot get away from town for more than a few hours he is often to be seen tramping the downs around Epsom and Dorking.

Victoria de los Angeles

THE somewhat fanciful stage name adopted by this celebrated soprano has given many people the impression that she was born in the Californian city that we associate with the film industry. She was, in fact, born in Barcelona in 1924, and her real name is Victoria Gamez Cima Lopez.

The family is of humble origin, the father having been employed as one of the caretakers of the University of Barcelona, and there is little evidence of any significant musical background. Nevertheless, as a child Victoria needed little encouragement to break into song, to the delight of her family and all who visited the little house near the University, but apparently without making any great impression upon the teachers at her primary school nearby. Her voice developed rapidly, and on leaving school she had little difficulty in being accepted as a singing student at the Barcelona Conservatory of Music.

Having spent much of her time in private study she was able to assimilate the course very quickly, and being exceptionally talented, was soon playing a prominent part in the various musical activities arranged to display the merits of the students. Apart from a successful but rather premature appearance in a production of Monteverdi's *Orfeo* at the age of eighteen, there is little to record until her proper début in Barcelona at the age of twenty. This was a lieder recital arranged by a local cultural organisation, and her success was such that she was able to begin her professional career almost immediately. Here was a really lovely voice, fresh with the bloom of youth, used in a manner that revealed not only a deep feeling for the words she sang but a surprisingly mature understanding of the intentions of the composers. A professor of the University who happened to be present declared: "Here is a real artist, not just another singer".

Even without that personal charm that can do so much for a young singer, and with which she is richly endowed, she could have established herself, for news of her "arrival" spread quickly in

16

musical circles, and she was soon to make her first tour of her native country.

The opera company at Barcelona's Teatro Liceo then invited her to play the part of the Countess in their forthcoming production of *The Marriage of Figaro*, and thus she made her début in opera in January 1945; another success that might have made her devote the whole of her time to the exciting realm of opera but for the many song recitals that had been arranged for her in Portugal as well as in Spain.

Nevertheless, the opera-lovers of Barcelona were to be the first to see her in some of the parts she portrayed so vividly in later years: Mimi in *La Bohème*, for instance, despite the fact that she looked anything but a frail little girl dying of consumption! Then there was her Marguerite in *Faust*, touchingly sympathetic, and her Elisabeth in *Tannhäuser*, sweetly and richly sung.

By modern standards, her performances in those days would be considered sadly lacking in dramatic intensity: her singing had to compensate for the immaturity of her acting. From what has been reported of those early days it seems that the audiences were so captivated by her voice that they willingly accepted the minimum of stage technique.

Refusing to concentrate solely upon opera, she continued her recital tours, and at the age of twenty-three won the first prize in the International Festival at Geneva. The effect of this was to extend her travels very considerably, and in 1948 she made her first visit to London. Her first engagement in this country was to sing in a broadcast performance of *La Vida Breve* (Manuel de Falla), and when one recalls what an outstanding event that was, it is not surprising that she has become one of our most regular visitors.

By 1950 she was well known in most European countries. In that year she made her American début at Carnegie Hall and also her first appearance at Covent Garden as Mimi. Further engagements in Canada, South America and even South Africa followed in quick succession, firmly establishing her reputation on both sides of the Atlantic.

Her début at the Metropolitan Opera House, New York, was made with the part of Marguerite in *Faust*, and although it was an undisputed success, many critical observers noticed that in this and in her interpretation of Cho-cho-San in *Madam Butterfly* that followed soon afterwards, she was dramatically weak and inclined to indulge in mannerisms. It was also remarked that her voice tended to be uneven.

However, when the American audiences saw and heard her as Mimi, they realised that she had put an enormous amount of very sympathetic study into the part, and warmly acclaimed her as one of the greatest interpreters of this rôle ever seen on the American stage. The heavily sentimental title rôle of *Manon* (Massenet), which gives the leading soprano some wonderful opportunities to display her gifts, proved as popular in New York in 1952 as it was at Covent Garden a year or so previously, and in 1953 she gave the American audiences a really magnificent performance of Marguerite.

She was now developing as a dramatic soprano in her own charming way, not by slavishly imitating the great singers of the past, but by trying to get right inside the personalities of the characters she was portraying, thus producing unconventional interpretations that always seemed to please and satisfy. This was observed by Mr. James Hinton Jnr., who wrote a most enthusiastic report of her Rosina (*Barber of Seville*) in the magazine *Opera*.[1] "The effect of Miss de los Angeles's Rosina is almost impossible to describe", he declared, "for she—almost literally—does nothing at all that is in the conventional sense 'effective'. She is rapidly becoming one of the great rarities so often talked about but so seldom met with: a personality who makes everyone believe in her characterizations".

Her ideas did not satisfy everybody, of course: there were some who, though acknowledging her musical integrity and the excellence of her voice, still considered that her acting was not wholly convincing. This was the case in 1953 when as Salud in *La Vida Breve* at the Holland Festival she distinguished herself musically but for some reason failed to portray the unfortunate gipsy girl convincingly. The production of this opera was generally dull and lacking in imagination, and it is possible that she unwittingly became imbued with the producer's mediocre ideas. A pity, because she loves Spanish music and this part could easily be one of her best.

Other operatic rôles in which Victoria de los Angeles has achieved eminence include Micaela in *Carmen*, Eva in *The Mastersingers*, and Mélisande in *Pelléas et Mélisande* (Debussy) but it must not be imagined that she has been working exclusively in the opera house during the past few years: she has distinguished herself as a concert

[1] June, 1954.

artist and as a recitalist, with clear understanding of Mozart, Handel, Schubert and Brahms as well as the Spanish composers. During her visit to England in 1957 there was ample evidence of her artistic maturity. In the *Daily Telegraph,* John Warrack wrote: "Madam Butterfly is the youngest and perhaps the most touching of Puccini's child-heroines. Even the problems of an actress playing Juliet are less than those of a singer who tackles this rôle, with its tiny, dwarfed innocence growing through betrayal to a tragic stature that suddenly towers above everyone else on the stage. Victoria de los Angeles. . . . concentrated on the purely vocal art of the rôle. Her pure, creamy tone was almost instrumental in its steadiness, yet of a melting human warmth—demure at the start, rapturous in the love duet, with its happy little sigh of 'E felice', strong and vibrant as Butterfly takes, at the end, a braver decision than anyone else in the opera has found possible".

Reporting her recital at the Festival Hall, London, the same newspaper declared: "Victoria de los Angeles has always been an incomparable interpreter of Spanish songs and more recently she has unmistakably conquered the French field. The German lied has somehow eluded her hitherto. But at the Festival Hall last night her singing of Schubert's *An die Musik*, Schumann's *Der Nussbaum*, and Brahms's *Das Mädchen Spricht* showed that here too she has now achieved an astonishing success. She manages the German language with a new ease and sensibility, achieves almost imperceptible transitions from one tonal colour to another, and phrases with a rightness which now seems instinctive. Her Spanish songs included, beside the well-loved Granados, lighter pieces by Vives and Obradors, in which the rather brighter colour of her voice and her dramatic experience found a new and wholly enchanting expression. Perhaps even so the gem of the evening was Delibes' *Bonjour, Suzon*, in which timing, characterisation and tone-quality were nothing less than perfect".

There can be little doubt that her voice like her artistry, has matured gracefully while still retaining the bloom and freshness of youth. The lower and middle part of her voice has that smooth, golden tone that every singer seeks, and at the same time possesses warmth, clarity and flexibility. Her upper notes are clear and pure but are apt to lose their velvety tone when in operatic work she has to deliver them *forte* across an orchestra. This hardening of the timbre is of course a problem that has worried generations of singers and to a great extent is inevitable: one cannot sing like a nightingale across an artillery of woodwind and brass. It also accounts for the ruin of many of the less robust voices in our opera houses, though in recent years there have been signs that some conductors are beginning to realise their responsibilities in this direction.

Victoria de los Angeles may be heard in several recordings of operas, including *The Barber of Seville* (ALP 1022-4), *Madam Butterfly* (ALP 1215-7), *La Bohème* (ALP 1409-10), *Manon* (ALP 1394-7), *Pagliacci* (ALP 1126-8), *Faust* (ALP 1162-5), and *La Vida Breve* (ALP 1150-1), but for those who do not want complete operas, there are many delightful recordings of excerpts. She has also recorded an agreeable recital of Spanish songs with guitar accompaniment (ALP 1063), of Spanish songs with instrumental ensemble in the Gothic, Renaissance and Baroque periods (ALP 1393) and a variety of other songs, too numerous to give in detail here, on other HMV discs.

She was married in 1948 to Enrique Magrina Mir, an impresario, and in private life delights in being an ordinary domesticated housewife. Her extensive travels have made her far less cosmopolitan than the average prima donna: she is still a typical Spanish woman, and would hate to be considered otherwise.

Trevor Anthony

THIS little biography of one of our finest young basses opens in the Amman Valley, at the village of Ty Croes, where Trevor Anthony was born. He inherited his parents' great love of music, but in his childhood had little opportunity of studying it except, of course, by going to evening classes and taking part in all the choral activities in the neighbourhood. At the age of fourteen he went with most of his schoolfellows into the coal mines.

By the time he was nineteen his voice had developed so well that he decided to take lessons from Gwilym R. Jones, conductor of the Ammanford Choral Society and a well-known musical personality in that part of the country. After two years with this teacher he entered for the Royal National Eisteddfod of Wales at Neath in 1934 and won the bass solo prize, creating a record by being the youngest singer ever to win that particular award. He sang excerpts from the Bach Mass in B minor, and drew high praise from the adjudicators, Plunket Greene and Dr. Morgan Lloyd.

A year later he won a singing scholarship to the Royal Academy of Music, and Mr. G. R. Jones with Mr. D. Jefferies, the agent of the great anthracite collieries in which he was working, called together a little committee of prominent local people to promote a fund for his maintenance as a student. Some idea of the spirit of comradeship there is in these mining localities may be gained from the fact that men from every colliery in the district contributed to the fund—and it must be remembered that in those days coal miners were poorly paid. In due course a presentation concert was arranged, and Trevor Anthony was given a cheque for nearly two hundred pounds.

So he came to London in 1935—with the scars of coal-mining still upon his arms. It requires little imagination to realize how strange he felt. The contrast between life in a mining village in the company of very homely folk and a studentship in London, with its restless scurrying millions of all nationalities, was vivid indeed. At home, music had been a simple, placid affair of singing the *Messiah* and other dearly-loved oratorios, favourite songs and airs handed down from father to son. In London, music seemed a vastly complicated art with its knights and doctors, exalted composers and learned professors, wealthy practitioners and pseudo-intellectuals, cranks and neurotics, "schools of thought" and whatnot. There were effeminate youths babbling about Schönberg, girls gushing about Stravinsky, organists rhapsodizing about pedal reeds, violinists arguing about Wieniawski, people who knew everything, people for whom Art was All.

It was a trifle bewildering, to say the least, but Trevor Anthony had the good fortune to come under the influence of Norman Allin, who had just accepted a professorship at the Academy. In this splendid singer he found not only a professor who would teach him like a father, but one of the best friends he had ever known. Half-an-hour of Allin's commonsense was sufficient to put him at his ease concerning all the humbug that was being prattled by the more irresponsible type of musician, and he soon discovered that there were plenty of people studying music—particularly at the Academy—who thought intelligently about Mozart, Bach and Brahms, and who did not sigh ecstatically at the very mention of some obscure contemporary composer.

Anthony's course at the Academy (of which he became a Fellow in 1952) was a long one, and included the study of the piano, of harmony and allied subjects. Living in London, even in those easygoing days, was not at all cheap, and by 1937 he was feeling most concerned at the very small amount left in his maintenance fund. Norman Allin assured him that somehow, sufficient funds would be found to keep him at the Academy, but fortunately, no appeal to anyone's generosity became necessary, for later in that year a vacancy for a bass singer occurred at Westminster Abbey. As soon as Dr. Bullock (the organist of the Abbey at that time) heard Anthony he accepted him, despite the fact that this promising young student knew very little of the highly specialized repertoire of the Abbey choir. This appointment solved Anthony's financial problem entirely.

He stayed at the Academy until 1939, arranging his lessons to fit in with his work at the Abbey. The latter was a great joy to him, and he readily acknowledges that it was in itself a musical education. Looking back over those years he recalls one or two amusing

TREVOR ANTHONY

experiences. During one of the services a few loose potash tablets in
his pocket somehow came into contact with a box of matches, and
to the amazement of everybody, his clothing caught alight. Fellow
lay-vicars beat at his cassock and surplice with copies of music to
put out the flames, and prevented any serious damage, but Anthony
had to retire to the vestry in haste, and there he discovered that a
substantial part of his clothing was ruined.

He also recalls the great service of thanksgiving held in the Abbey
for the safe return of King George VI and Queen Elizabeth
from Canada. On the previous evening he had indulged in a little
boxing match with one of his brothers and acquired a fearful black-
eye. This was just in its most colourful stage on the following day
when members of the Government and half of Debrett were sitting
in full view of the choir stalls.

In 1940 Sir Henry J. Wood heard him quite by chance and
engaged him for a promenade concert. Alas! the Queen's Hall was
reduced to a heap of rubble before this could be fulfilled. However,
a variety of other attractive engagements were then coming his way
—chiefly to appear as soloist with leading choral societies—and he
had every reason for feeling that he had "arrived".

His calling-up papers "arrived" too, and to have to sit down and
cancel half-a-dozen future bookings was a decided anti-climax. It
was perhaps a small consolation that he had been given the service
of his choice: the Royal Navy. For the next six years he was a
member of the Senior Service as a wireless telegraphist. Most of his
time was spent in convoy work, and he had several thrilling
experiences. He was in one of the ships of the convoy that fought its
way to Malta in 1942 against terrible odds, when we suffered
extremely heavy losses, including that of the Aircraft-carrier *Eagle*.
Later, he was invalided from duties at sea and spent the rest of the
time at shore stations.

On his return to the Abbey choir, Anthony decided that the first
thing to do in picking up the threads of his musical career was to go
to Norman Allin for a refresher course. Then the choral societies
began offering him engagements again, and in the following year he
made his first appearance at a promenade concert under the direction of Sir Adrian Boult. By the summer of 1946 his services were
so much in demand in various parts of the country that he was
obliged to relinquish his appointment at the Abbey,

Then came a pleasant surprise: an invitation to sing before Sir Thomas Beecham. As a result of this he was chosen to sing the part of King Mark in the broadcast performance of *Tristan and Isolde* which Beecham gave with stars of the Metropolitan Opera House, New York, in the following October. The eminent conductor was evidently deeply impressed by his singing, because early in 1947 he chose Anthony again to record the bass solos in the *Messiah* for the Victor Company of America. This was done at the H.M.V. studios in London. In the same year he made his first appearance at the Leeds Triennial Festival, when he took part in the Bach Mass in B minor.

In 1949 he joined the Covent Garden Opera Company, and shortly afterwards had the distinction of singing with Kirsten Flagstad in *The Ring*, despite the fact that he had, at that time, very little experience in opera. Later, he became associated with the English Opera Group, playing the leading baritone part in *The Rape of Lucretia* when they visited Germany recently. His principal activity, however, is now in oratorio work, which takes him all over the country. He is one of the soloists in the H.M.V. recording of the *Messiah* with the Luton Choral Society and Royal Philharmonic Orchestra under Sir Thomas Beecham (ALP 1077-80), and in *The Little Sweep* (Act 3 of *Let's make an opera*) by Benjamin Britten (Decca LXT 5163).

Trevor Anthony feels that the necessity of earning a living in music is forcing many of our singers to exploit their voices unreasonably: they have to undertake such a variety of engagements that it is impossible to specialize in the particular sphere of work for which their voices happen to be suited. The young soloist of today finds himself singing the *Messiah* one evening in Newcastle, playing in *Rigoletto* in London the next night, and the following day tearing off to Birmingham for a recital. The physical strain is bad enough, but the lack of time to study and specialize in any one class of work is even more serious.

Anthony is deeply interested in Welsh culture, and loves reading the poetry of his native land. He believes that the earlier forms of Welsh poetry are eminently suitable for setting to music.

The wealth of musical talent in Wales offers great posibilities, he declares, and he feels strongly that the National Orchestra of Wales which did such splendid work under Warwick Braithwaite, should

TREVOR ANTHONY

be revived and made truly representative of the *whole* of Wales. It
could be employed admirably in support of all the choral societies in
Wales, and could give regular orchestral concerts in the towns and
larger villages. There is a great need for a National Orchestra in
Wales, and he hopes that influential people in his native land will
now make a special effort to re-establish this ensemble.

In the provinces, especially, he has found a disturbing tendency
to overlook the importance of the art of accompanying. People
arranging concerts will often go to the expense of engaging a first-
class singer or instrumentalist and then try to economize by allowing a mediocre local pianist to act as accompanist. The result is that
the soloist is never at his ease, and even if the performance is not
marred by wrong notes, it seldom comes up to expectations. We
must get rid of the notion that "anybody can accompany".

There are not enough young faces in the choral societies at the
present time, and Mr. Anthony fears that the influence of dance
music, television and the cinema, is chiefly responsible for the
decline of interest in choral singing. There is too much ready-made
entertainment, and consequently it requires a good deal of effort to
get young people to take part in music-making. The Arts Council is
doing great work, but Anthony feels that it should have the support,
or be part of, a nation-wide organization co-ordinating all forms of
musical activity.

He is a strong believer in daily exercises to keep the voice in good
form, but rarely sings them for more than about ten minutes at a
time. His taste in music is not conservative, and he is as interested
in symphonic and chamber music as in anything for the voice. In
song, his preference is for German lieder because of the wonderful
scope that this type of vocal music offers to the singer. He deplores
the lack of good modern bass songs, and hopes that some of our
young composers will consider writing more frequently for his class
of voice.

Trevor Anthony is a cheerful, stocky figure; enthusiastic, and
very good natured. Because he is a nature-lover, a walk in the
country—or even a train journey through a rural scene—is an
uplifting experience. But his greatest joy is to explore the wilder
stretches of the Welsh coast: he will sit for hours listening to the
eternal rumbling of the sea, watching the ever-changing pattern of
the sky, and pondering upon many things; for it can be stated quite
frankly that he is a deeply religious man; one who has thought

25

seriously about the problems of today and has come to the conclusion that only by the Christian way of life can one find true peace and happiness. He has also the Welshman's love of antiquities, and nothing pleases him more than when his travels take him near old buildings, castles and cathedrals.

He was married in 1941 to Olga Bonnell, a South Wales schoolteacher. They have one son, Robert, aged eleven, now at a preparatory school in North London.

Isobel Baillie

TO those of us who delight in vocal purity and stability, Isobel Baillie's voice is one of the loveliest in the world today. One cannot help thinking that if she had been born in Vienna and endowed with less of the charming modesty that is one of her outstanding characteristics, she would probably have been acclaimed an international celebrity at least twenty years ago. As it is, her rise to eminence was comparatively slow: the result of a great deal of hard work, a fact of which she has every reason to be proud. It can be truly said that few singers could have accomplished more, or given greater pleasure to millions of British music lovers, than she has during the past twenty years.

Isobel Baillie was born at Hawick, in Scotland, on 9 March 1895, but has spent the greater part of her life in Manchester. She began singing very early in life, and at the age of six was appearing in little concerts at Newcastle, where her family was then living. No great attention was given to her voice, however, until some years later. When she was about twelve years old she was attending a school in Manchester, where it was customary to assemble all the children in the main hall for a closing hymn at the end of the day's lessons. One afternoon, her teacher happened to hear her singing this hymn with the other girls and was so struck by the beauty of her voice that she told her to sing the next verse alone, so that the headmaster could hear what a promising young singer he had in his care. He was very favourably impressed and it was chiefly due to his efforts on her behalf that Isobel Baillie began to study music seriously.

A scholarship took her to a local High School, and during the next few years she thought a great deal about music as a career. Opportunities to enter the musical profession were then far fewer than at the present time, and although she told her headmistress of her determination to become a professional singer when she left school, she had to go into an office for a few years while the foundations of her career were being laid. It will be observed that she had no "silver spoon" of any kind to help her.

When she was about fifteen she became a pupil of Madame Sadler-Fogg, mother of the late Eric Fogg, the conductor, and it was this able teacher who launched her professionally. Typical of Isobel Baillie's thoroughness is the fact that she continued her lessons long after her début. A few years later, Sir Hamilton Harty advised her to study in Italy for a while, so she went to Milan and became a pupil of Somma.

During those few years in business she sang at many concerts in the Manchester area, but as soon as she was able to devote the whole of her time to singing she began to go much further afield—to more distant parts of Lancashire and Yorkshire at first, and then, in time, to musical centres all over Great Britain.

Her first broadcast was made before the BBC station was opened in Manchester: she went in 1922 to the Metropolitan-Vickers works at Trafford Park and made her radio début in an experimental studio. Those were the days when we scratched a crystal with a "cat's-whisker" and felt extremely proud of our home-made apparatus when a distant voice sounded in the headphones.

Miss Baillie's first important concert was with the Hallé Orchestra under Sir Hamilton Harty in 1923, and for twenty-five years she has been closely associated with this organization. Even if this is not a record it is certainly a matter for congratulation on both sides.

In the same year, 1923, she made her début in London. A friend urged William Boosey to give her an audition, and after hearing her he immediately recommended her to Sir Henry J. Wood. A good voice was never lost upon Sir Henry, and after a short audition he booked her for a promenade concert in the forthcoming season. Since then she has appeared in almost every promenade season and won the affection of countless millions who have learned to love good music at those ever-popular concerts.

In 1933 Isobel Baillie crossed the Atlantic for the first time, and had the honour of being the first British artist to sing at the famous Hollywood Bowl. Sir Hamilton Harty was the conductor on this occasion. On her way, she was introduced to a New York concert agent who consented to hear her provided that she would pay the expenses of the audition. This was rather a surprising request, but she agreed, and gave a splendid little private recital to him and a number of *entrepreneurs* of his acquaintance. All the latter congratulated her heartily, but did nothing because in those days she hadn't a "big name". The agent who had arranged the audition proceeded to book two engagements for her: one in Vancouver and the other in Nova Scotia without even bothering to consult her! He evidently imagined that the privilege of singing on his side of the Atlantic would compensate her for the colossal waste of time and money in making a special journey from England to Nova Scotia, and then crossing the entire breadth of Canada to sing at Vancouver! When she explained the impossibility of doing this, and the fact that it would mean the cancellation of many important engagements in England, the people at Nova Scotia understood perfectly, and willingly released her from the obligation. Those responsible for the concert at Vancouver, however, demanded the payment of £100 damages, despite the fact that she had signed nothing personally. Miss Baillie felt that, strictly speaking, they were entitled to some sort of compensation for her agent's hastiness, and actually paid them the sum demanded. This little story is told so that ambitious young singers may accept it as a warning!

When Toscanini came to London in 1937 he gave her an audition and was particularly charmed by her voice. Speaking about her afterwards, he said "She sings right in the middle of the note" and then using his hands to indicate the sort of wobble one finds in many sopranos' voices, added: "with none of this". He engaged her for Brahms' *Requiem*, which he conducted in May of that year at the London Music Festival, and at two concerts in the following year she sang in the Beethoven Ninth Symphony under his baton.

In 1940 Miss Baillie went on a tour of New Zealand with the late Gladys Ripley, Heddle Nash and Oscar Natzke, the New Zealand bass. They crossed the Atlantic without a convoy. On this tour, which included a large number of important concerts, Isobel Baillie made her first appearance in opera—as Marguerite in *Faust*—and was a tremendous success.

With Gladys Ripley, Miss Baillie then returned to England, and arrived at Liverpool to find a "blitz" in progress. She had to wait five hours on the quay for a taxi, and when she eventually got home to Manchester she found that the German bombers were concentrated there as well, and she spent her first night in an air-raid shelter. This was scarcely the sort of home-coming she had anticipated.

Of her great work in wartime, in which she did innumerable performances for E.N.S.A. without charging a single fee, much could be written, but it must suffice to say that she made extensive tours of army camps, airfields and naval stations giving classical recitals that were highly appreciated. In the summer of 1945 she made a tour of the continent to entertain the allied troops in various countries, travelling from one camp to another by air. She also made an extensive tour of South Africa in 1952, and has toured New Zealand twice.

Because she has always enjoyed learning new works, her repertoire is extensive, and includes almost every oratorio sung in this country in which there is a soprano part. All the great works of Handel appeal strongly to her, and she particularly loves *The Kingdom* (Elgar) and Brahms' *Requiem*. But she also takes a keen interest in the works of contemporary composers, and is proud to have sung in the first performance of such works as Dyson's *Canterbury Pilgrims* (at Winchester) and *Quo Vadis*. Miss Baillie has noted that there is nowadays more demand for the lesser-known works and a willingness to try to understand modern music. In connection with the latter she says that a work must speak to her as *music*, otherwise she is not interested in it. "I am not concerned with mere cleverness."

Her recordings—chiefly for Columbia—are also too numerous to mention in detail, but it might be said that one of her favourites is *The Blessed Virgin's Expostulation* (Purcell) made with Arnold Goldsborough at the organ. Her voice is certainly extremely beautiful in this particular recording, and it is also heard to advantage in her fine recordings of the *Messiah* and *Elijah*, as well as in arias from Handel's *Solomon* and *Samson*. Who could fail to be impressed by her exquisitely clear and sweet tone in *Let the Bright Seraphim* (from Handel's *Samson*), for instance? Every note in the long runs is perfectly sounded and as true as a bell. Could any voice be more appropriately angelic? Many people have expressed their delight in the purity of her "choirboy" voice, but few have stopped to consider the most remarkable feature of it: that after thirty years of constant use it has a vernal freshness, a youthful bloom that is the envy of thousands of young singers still in their "teens". What is her secret? Many hundreds of singers have asked that question and we shall see in a moment that she is guided by a few quite simple rules of singing; but before we pass on to her views upon voice production, a word must be said about another characteristic of this lovely voice: its ethereal serenity. To hear her in Brahms' *Requiem*, or in *I know that my Redeemer liveth*, is an uplifting experience that leaves one with a sense of joyful tranquility and a realization of the mission of music upon earth. Her long-playing recordings include two Mendelssohn songs, *Greeting* and *I would that my love* (sed 5526), and she may be heard in the Decca recording of Vaughan Williams's *Sea Symphony* (LXT 2907-8).

Isobel Baillie firmly believes that it is useless to become a singer merely because you have a good voice: you must be willing to go through years of hard training, and to find your happiness in the effort. A professional singer's career is one of the most strenuous you can choose, and unless you really love the work, with its trials and disappointments as well as its joyful achievements, it is better left alone.

One of the tragedies of singing is the number of young people with good voices who enter the profession ill-equipped—lacking the fundamental knowledge of how to use and preserve a voice. After a few years their voices are worn out or have degenerated into something decidedly unpleasant, with distressing quality and a "wobble" as well.

The art of singing can be acquired only from a responsible singing teacher, and it is not much use to prescribe any set of general rules, but there are a few basic principles that Isobel Baillie has always borne in mind and which she is pleased to pass on to those who are on the threshold of singing careers. The most important, perhaps, can be summarized in the words: "If it doesn't feel right, it isn't right". If a phrase cannot be sung with perfect ease, it is better not sung at all, for strain will show in the quality of the singing and is liable to impair the voice.

Secondly, Isobel Baillie has never used her voice to its utmost capacity. She believes that "going all out" is a great mistake that is bound to result in signs of wear and tear in the voice before long. It is of course a great temptation when one is apt to be carried away at a musical climax, but a good artist should be able to produce that "last ounce" effect without actually spending the last ounce!

Similarly, one should never exploit the extremes of one's compass. Her own range is approximately B to top C—just over two octaves—but she would not dream of singing a high C if she could not sing at least a tone above without strain.

She is a firm believer in singing "from the heart and diaphragm" and not merely from the brain and throat.

Finally, she would remind young singers that many modern songs are really duets for soloist and accompanist. The accompaniment nowadays is generally a significant part of the song, not merely a convenient background for the soloist: therefore the singer should understand it. Unfortunately, when modern songs fail to make the desired impression it is frequently not the fault of the singer: the accompanist is just as apt to under-rate his responsibility in the "duet".

In private life, Isobel Baillie is absolutely unaffected by her great success as a singer. After a concert tour she enjoys nothing more than to be able to spend a quiet spell at her Hampshire home with her husband and daughter, and a casual caller would probably find her in the kitchen with her sleeves rolled up enjoying an hour's cooking! She excels in the culinary art, and holds very sensible views about its importance.

She is also quite a connoisseur of Chinese art and lustre china, and has many fine specimens in her possession.

Kenelm Harvey

Norman Allin

PLATE II

Norman Allin: Sketch by
Tom Purvis

PLATE III

Trevor Anthony

PLATE V

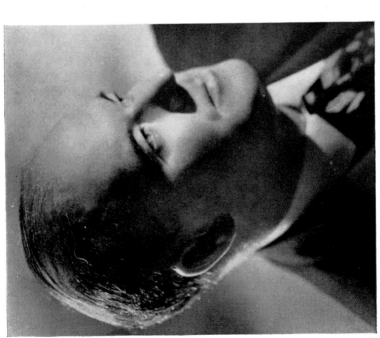

Bruce Boyce

Vandamme

PLATE IV

Bruce Boyce

FEW British vocalists in recent years have risen to any significant degree of eminence as lieder singers because the majority of them have been obliged either to carry on business as "general practitioners" in singing or to seek regular, well-paid positions in the various opera companies. Those who undertake miscellaneous work generally find themselves too busy tearing up and down the country fulfilling engagements with provincial choral societies to devote much time to the study of lieder, and those whose inclinations are mainly in the direction of the opera house usually discover that their work puts upon their voice just about as much strain as it will stand.

To become a lieder singer of any importance, one has to learn to say "no" to offers of engagements which do not really suit one's voice, and that requires a tremendous amount of will-power unless one happens to possess a considerable private income. Many a singer has risked damage to his voice simply to pay next quarter's rent. One must also spend a great deal of time in patient study and frequently risk much of one's savings in giving recitals in which artistic success does not necessarily mean pecuniary reward for all the effort involved.

Because the way of the lieder singer can so often be hard and stony, the achievements of Bruce Boyce, therefore, deserve more than a passing word of praise. He has of course done a variety of work during the past decade or so, but his devotion to the art of lieder singing has never flagged, and today he is one of the few British singers who can command respect in this exacting field of work when touring the continent of Europe.

His life story is refreshingly original. He was born in London, Ontario, in 1910, son of a Canadian veterinary surgeon who, metaphorically if not literally, had not a note of music in his head. As a boy he found great pleasure in singing, especially when his mother, who had an excellent voice, would join him in a duet.

While he was quite small, his family left Canada and settled at

Superior, a small town in Nebraska, an area commonly referred to by Americans as the Middle West. Here, in an environment one would scarcely describe as auspicious for the rearing of lieder singers, he went to school. It so happened that the senior school he attended had on its staff a lady teacher who possessed a flair for producing Shakespeare, musical plays and concerts, and his pleasant singing voice was soon discovered. These activities at school stimulated his interest in music and poetry, but certainly did not lead him to music as a profession.

On leaving school at seventeen he went to California "in search of adventure"—with very little money in his pocket and only the vaguest ideas about what he would like to do for a living. In these days of so-called "full employment" with the State for ever trying to grade, classify and mould the younger generation, it might seem oddly romantic for a lad to leave home in search of adventure in this manner, but the Americans, particularly in those days, thought nothing of it. He went to the farms for the fruit-picking and grain-harvesting, took odd jobs here and there and gradually assessed the opportunities that life had to offer. He decided eventually to try to get to Cornell University, where his father had been, and to get the money he worked all the harder, saving every dollar he could spare.

Like many American youths, he paid his way through University by working at menial jobs in the evenings. Most of his spare time was spent in washing cars at night in a very large garage, and it was here, by singing to keep up his spirits, that he became aware of the potentiality of his fine baritone voice. He joined the Glee Club at Cornell, and Mr. Eric Dudley, its director, suggested that he should consider singing as a career. He had started at Cornell as a medical student, but on receiving this advice from so able a musician, he changed over to an arts course to study languages and music. Life at the University soon became very exciting, with its varied musical activities in which he frequently distinguished himself as a soloist, and in his last year there he had the honour of being invited to the White House to entertain some of the President's guests. He stayed at the White House for three days and gave two after-dinner recitals.

During the vacations he invariably went to a mountain resort with a professional quartet to entertain at a club, and he might well have continued this type of activity had he not won a scholarship in 1934 that provided him with the means to study music abroad.

But for the bawlings of the two notorious dictators, he would probably have gone either to Germany or to Italy, but he decided instead to come to London to study with Reinhold von Warlich, who was dividing his time between London, Paris and Salzburg. As a private pupil of this famous teacher he discovered the joy of lieder singing, and he resolved to make this his principal activity. He gave his first London recital at the old Grotrian Hall in 1936: a memorable debut that marked the commencement of his career in London—recitals every year and many oratorio and broadcast engagements —though it was not until after the Second World War that he became the prominent figure we know so well today. This is perhaps because the years preceding the war were spent partly in this country and partly in America. In 1937 and 1938 he gave recitals at the Town Hall, New York, and was beginning to establish himself as a celebrity in the United States when the outbreak of war temporarily stopped his work. He was in America when that country came into the war, and enlisted in the American Army Air Force.

The latter years of the war were spent in London, not as a musician but as a member of the U.S. Air Transport Headquarters, and in those days there was little time for singing. On being demobilised in 1946 he decided to make his home in London, mainly because it often costs a great deal of money to establish oneself as a celebrity in America, whereas in this country even those with slender means can get a foothold if they possess merit. Two Wigmore Hall recitals marked the resumption of his professional career, and in but a little while he had re-established himself as a recitalist and oratorio soloist.

He had always been interested in opera, and in 1947 he accepted an invitation to sing certain suitable roles in the season of Italian Opera that was about to start at the Cambridge Theatre. Before this venture collapsed financially, he distinguished himself in the title rôle of *Don Giovanni* (forty performances), as the elderly Count Monterone in *Rigoletto* and as Marcel in *La Bohème*.

For several years after this he did a much greater variety of work than he usually attempts nowadays. He played the Count in *Figaro* under Kleiber at Covent Garden; he was associated with the English Opera Group for some years; he undertook various operatic rôles on the continent and did several performances with the London Opera Club. At the same time he was carrying out many oratorio assignments, notably in the *St. Matthew Passion*, a work for which he has a very deep feeling and in which he can usually be heard at his best, and in Vaughan Williams's *Sea Symphony*.

Bruce Boyce is a real baritone, and for that reason does not attempt parts which can better be sung by a bass. His range is about two octaves (F—F, but he has managed a top A flat in the past!). It is a rich and flexible voice with the fine gradations of tone that are so essential in lieder work. Reporting a recital he gave early in May 1957, one of the *Daily Telegraph* critics wrote: "Bruce Boyce enhanced his already high reputation with a Schubert recital at Wigmore Hall yesterday that was both intelligently planned and excellently performed. The ground plan was a song from each of Schubert's creative years, starting with the *Klaglied* of 1812 and ending with five of the *Schwanengesang*, among them the last song of all, *Die Taubenpost*. Mr. Boyce showed that he has in him much of the true art of the Lieder singer. His voice was basically strong and roundly masculine: it was superbly robust. He could vary and explore moods with a sure touch, following the great *Prometheus* with a complete contrast in *Die Sterne* and succeeding with both. The climax of a rewarding afternoon was a really superb performance of *Der Doppelgänger*. Gerald Moore contributed a large measure of the recital's success."

His affection for Schubert, Wolf, Brahms and Schumann does not tempt him to neglect the merits of other composers, and it is significant that he has the greatest admiration for many English composers, especially Vaughan Williams, Herbert Howells and John Ireland. In Ivor Gurney (1890-1937) he sees a composer whose sensitive works have been unwarrantably neglected.

Bruce Boyce has a most modest and humble approach to his art and is concerned at the attitude of some of our younger singers today who expect to become international celebrities almost as soon as they leave one of the colleges: they do not bother to learn from other artists—listening to the radio or gramophone records at home is not sufficient—and do not seem to realise that there is quite a lot to know even about platform technique. He urges young singers not to be afraid to get second or third opinions about vocal problems and to distrust cranks who claim to have special "methods". In music, he declares, "a broad outlook is necessary: don't harbour preconceived notions about art".

He has recorded three fine recitals for Oiseau-Lyre (Schubert,

OL 50045; Brahms, OL 50044; Wolf, OL 50026) and took part in the same company's recording of Purcell's ode for the birthday of the Queen (*Come ye sons of art:* DL 53004), the Monteverdi *Vespers* (OL 50021-2), the Lully *Miserere* (DL 53003) and Handel's *Apollo e Dafne* (OL 50038). For Philips he has recorded *Sea Drift* (Delius: ABL 3088), and took part in the Decca recording of *Elijah* (LXT 5000-2).

Mr. Boyce was married to Miss Joy Egerton in 1949 and at home is the conventional gardener-handyman. He collects etchings (being partially colour-blind, oils and water-colours make no great appeal to him) and antiques as far as the soaring prices of today will permit. His only other recreation is an occasional evening at the theatre.

Owen Brannigan

AS his name suggests, Owen Brannigan is of Irish descent, but he was born in Northumberland—at Annitsford, near Newcastle—and given a Welsh Christian name! He feels that if he could now discover some connection with Scotland, he would be complete. (He could of course follow the example of the man who wanted a commission in a famous Scottish regiment that stipulated either residence or the ownership of property north of the border. The applicant sent a pair of old flannels to a famous firm of cleaners in Perth and then reported, quite truthfully, that he owned property in Scotland.)

As a boy, Brannigan had a pleasant soprano voice which he used to advantage in the choir of a nearby Catholic church, of which his father was the organist. One of his "heroes" in those days was an uncle with a magnificent bass voice, and he was determined that when he grew up he would emulate him, so with this incentive, and his father's encouragement, he took his music seriously.

As a reward for doing well in a pianoforte examination at the age of twelve, his father took him to see his first opera: the Carl Rosa Company's production of *The Bohemian Girl* at Newcastle. How vividly he remembers that thrilling excursion, particularly as in their excitement they missed the last train home. His father had to make the return journey on foot carrying his far-from-light son on his back!

At school, Owen was given the job of playing the piano while his fellow-pupils marched into the assembly hall, and was frequently called upon for a song at concerts, which enabled him to shine as brightly indoors as he did upon the football field.

On leaving school, he was apprenticed in the joiner's shop at a local colliery, and as soon as his musical abilities were discovered he was billed to appear at a colliery social. Although he was then a big lad of nearly sixteen, his voice had not yet broken, and when at this event he mounted the platform and started to sing soprano he caused quite a sensation.

38

OWEN BRANNIGAN

A few weeks later his voice was gone, so his father removed him from the choir and gave him the much less glamorous job of pumping the organ! He made no attempt to sing for two or three years, but spent his days in becoming a good craftsman and his evenings in studying music.

At nineteen, Owen Brannigan decided that his bass voice was sufficiently stabilized to be used in public, and he joined two good male voice choirs: the Bebside and the Cranlington. With these keen amateurs he got plenty of vocal exercise in good company, and nothing could have pleased him more than when a year or two ago both choirs invited him to return as soloist at one of their concerts.

Most of his evenings were now spent in preparing himself for the various little solo engagements that came his way, and he was making headway as a semi-professional in the north when the great depression of 1929 compelled him to come south in search of a job. He was then a skilled joiner, and proud of his trade.

With sufficient money for only a single ticket he came to London and stayed for a while with some friends at Slough, finding employment locally. As soon as he had settled down he joined the Windsor Operatic Society and was told that as his voice had great possibilities, he ought to have it trained by a really competent teacher. Following this advice, he went to William Barrand, a member of the Eton College choir, who gave him regular lessons.

Brannigan's work then took him to London as foreman for a firm of contractors, and the move gave him an opportunity of studying at the Guildhall School of Music in the evenings. He took singing lessons from Walter Hyde and worked at elocution under Cairns James; while Jennie Hyman acted as his *répétiteur*. In the opera class he made such a good impression that he was given a scholarship, and during the next few years he was to win almost every prize the school could offer, including the gold medal and the medal of the Worshipful Company of Musicians.

In those exhausting days it was sheer enthusiasm that drove him on: he used to leave his work at five o'clock and go straight to the Guildhall School to study and rehearse until ten every night of the week! Being of good physique he was able to stand the strain, even when he was taking leading parts in the students' opera productions.

When the time came for him to take up singing professionally he had risen to the position of building manager, and the giving up of his job was not a matter to be treated lightly. However, in 1938 he received an appointment as a bass singer at Westminster Cathedral, and this helped to tide him over the difficult period of transition.

In the following year he had an audition at the BBC and within a week Stanford Robinson had given him a part in a broadcast production of *Hugh the Drover*. This was the first of over thirty engagements he was to receive in broadcast opera and also led to a good deal of other work for the BBC. By 1940 he was sufficiently well established to relinquish his post at Westminster Cathedral.

The next milestone in his career was reached when in 1941 he was invited to become a principal bass at Sadler's Wells. He joined the company, which was then on tour, and found that his first assignment was to appear as Sarastro in a production of *The Magic Flute* in Birmingham. He recalls that on his first night he was so nervous that he thought he would fall into the orchestra pit! In the same week he had to play the part of Colline in *La Bohème*. They could scarcely have expected more from a new member in his first week, even in wartime, when exacting demands were made of those who were trying to carry on the nation's musical life. Brannigan's success in these two rôles proved that the company had made a valuable acquisition, and throughout the remainder of the war years he stayed with them playing both in London and the provincial centres, and also doing as much general concert work as his duties would permit.

He went with the Sadler's Wells Company on their post-war tour of Germany and had some interesting experiences. At Lübeck, for instance, he had the honour of sharing a recital with Melchior, and gave some enthusiastically-received performances to the troops. At one of these he introduced a number of Northumbrian folk songs and was amazed when he was repaid by one of the greatest ovations he had ever received. He discovered after the concert that a strong contingent of the Royal Northumberland Fusiliers had been in the audience! Incidently, on his return to England his 'plane made a forced landing, which caused a rapid cooling-off in his keenness for air-travel.

After this tour he left the Sadler's Wells Company but arranged to appear with them from time to time as a guest artist. He readily acknowledges the help he has received from them, declaring: "I owe much of my experience to Sadler's Wells".

With freedom to do a wider range of work, Brannigan has been able to appear in the first production of *Peter Grimes* at both Sadler's Wells and Covent Garden, and of *The Rape of Lucretia* at Glyndebourne; he has played Dr. Bartolo in *Figaro* and Banquo in *Macbeth* (the latter before members of the Royal Family) at the 1947 Edinburgh Festival; he has made a hit as Alfonso in *Così fan Tutte* at Sadler's Wells and also fulfilled important oratorio engagements with some of our leading societies. He once appeared in a performance of *The Childhood of Christ* (Berlioz) under Sir Malcolm Sargent at two days' notice, and in January 1947 had yet another new experience: that of playing the part of Vertigo, the innkeeper, in a televised transmission of Offenbach's comic opera *Pepito*.

In oratorio, his preferences are for such works as the Bach Mass in B minor, the *Messiah, Creation* and *Elijah*, and whenever he is asked to give a song recital he likes to include one or two folksongs of his native Northumberland, of which he has made a speciality. Because of this he is sometimes described by his friends as Northumberland's "musical ambassador", and he often tells of an aged miner of his acquaintance who thinks so highly of these folksongs that he is apt to overlook the importance of all the rest of Brannigan's repertoire. When, for instance, "Branny" (as he is known to all his friends) told him that he had been engaged for an important performance of the Bach Mass in B minor, the old pitman's comment was: "Aye, but surely ye'll be puttin' some of yer own songs in?"

He can be heard as Mr. Peacham in the recording of Gay's setting of *The Beggar's Opera* conducted by Sir Malcolm Sargent (CLP 1052-3), and as the bass soloist in the *Messiah* (LXT 2921-4) and the *Tales of Hoffmann* (LXT 2582-4).

Owen Brannigan now seems to be in his prime: he can get down to a steady, powerful bottom C and yet soar to a top F without straining. He deplores the modern tendency to look upon a bass merely as a singer who can't sing high notes, and urges all young basses to concentrate upon developing a good compass by not neglecting the upper part of their voice in their enthusiasm to acquire an impressive bottom register. A heavy low D or C is thrilling and worth its weight in gold, as it were, but its value disappears if you cannot get engagements because of your inability to sing a top D. It should always be remembered that most modern composers make great demands on the highest notes of bass singers.

To those who wish to take up singing professionally Brannigan would say that it is useless to rely upon one good octave and a few indifferent notes at either end of it.

While he believes that operatic experience is of the utmost value to any type of singer, Brannigan has a healthy northcountry respect for the oratorios of Handel, which, he declares, provide ideal singing exercise and just the stimulation one needs to keep the voice in good form.

If he is young, the student need not be deterred by a seemingly-limited range. When Brannigan started he was unable to sing a top D, yet with careful practice he extended his voice upwards to what even many baritones regard as their limit. The secret is to sing carefully selected exercises—those with plenty of arpeggios—touching the highest notes very lightly at first. In time—unless the voice is by nature absolutely unadaptable—these high notes will get stronger and more stable. Exercises with little broken or repeated runs can also be helpful. The student must remember, however, that one should not claim to be able to sing a high note unless one can comfortably reach the note above; and similarly, one should not claim a low note unless a tone lower can be reached without difficulty. This little rule should be borne in mind when one is deciding whether or not a certain rôle can be attempted. Brannigan agrees with several of the other singers in this book that a "wobble" is generally the result of strain.

He thinks it is a pity that so many basses skip the trills in the works of such composers as Bach and Purcell. It is not easy to acquire the art of making a perfect trill with a heavy voice, but he has proved that it is quite possible, and recommends the following method of practising it: the two notes should first of all be sung alternately at a slow pace, taking care to get them even, and then the speed should be gradually increased until the alternation becomes a steady trill. It takes time, but is well worth while.

A pleasant and unassuming personality, Brannigan is interested in art as well as music, and frequently indulges in a little sketching, though he is extremely modest about his accomplishments in this direction. He is also a great lover of the immortal works of Dickens. A free day and a little sunshine will generally take him on to the golf course or send him off for a day's drive in the country.

Maria Meneghini Callas

A MOST remarkable voice, but one that does not appeal to all and which also seems to vary in quality at times, has made Maria Meneghini Callas one of the few great singers of today who follow in the old prima donna tradition.

This fine soprano is of Greek origin, her real surname being Calogeropoulos, though she was born in New York on December 3rd 1923. Her father was a pharmacist. Both of her parents were extremely interested in music and it was their love of opera, in particular, that aroused Maria's interest in singing at a very early age. She still recalls the tremendous thrill of going to an opera in her childhood, and it is not surprising to learn that she became quite a little "star" at school. Her music lessons began at the age of ten.

When she was thirteen her family returned to Athens, where she soon won a scholarship to the Royal Conservatory. Here, she became a pupil of that wonderfully dynamic Spanish soprano Elvira de Hildago, who found in her the sort of tractable, zealous and, above all, gifted pupil that every teacher dreams of training. Possessing already a sound basic knowledge of music, and quite unafraid of technical difficulties, the young singer worked as if her very existence depended upon achieving her ambition, and although she must have taxed her voice to the utmost in those arduous years, it stood up well under the strain: a sure sign of a God-given voice.

Maria was but fourteen years of age when she made her first important public appearance in opera: as Santuzza in *Cavalleria Rusticana*. Alas! she was just about to embark upon her career when the Second World War broke out and she found that the majority of the opportunities she had counted on had disappeared overnight. Her progress during the next five or six years was severely restricted, especially during the German occupation of Greece, though she was able to appear from time to time at the Opera House in Athens.

Her rise to fame was therefore comparatively slow, and she did not achieve international eminence until well after the war, her first notable appearance being in *La Gioconda* (Ponchielli) at Verona in August 1947. This performance was given not in an opera house but in an open-air arena, and one can well imagine that the singing of the title rôle in such circumstances was a formidable task that probably put a heavy strain upon her voice. Nevertheless, it was a triumph, and the conductor, Tullio Serafin, was so convinced that another great opera singer had "arrived" that he recommended her for the parts of Isolde and Turandot in Venice. These two engagements led to her being chosen for the title rôle of *Aïda* and for the part of Brünnhilde in *Die Walküre* in Turin.

It was at this stage in her career that she married Giovanni Meneghini, a wealthy Italian business man. They made their home in Italy, though much of their time was later to be spent in America and, of course, on the many tours that Madame Callas undertook in later years.

By 1950 she was recognised on both sides of the Atlantic, the year in which, after some gratifying successes in Buenos Aires and Mexico, she made her début at La Scala, Milan, as Aïda. In the following year she became a member of the company of that famous opera house and began her distinguished association with the Florence Music Festivals.

In England, she made her début at Covent Garden in 1952 singing the title-part in *Norma* (Bellini). She caused a veritable sensation, and even moved one of the more vinegary critics to remark: "Quite amazing. She reminded me of the days when singers could sing". Her triumphs at our own opera house were repeated in the following year, when she appeared as Aïda and as Leonora in *Il Trovatore*.

It was again as Norma that she captivated Chicago when she made her début there in 1954, and in the same city in the following year caused a furore as Elvira in Bellini's *I Puritani* and in the title rôle of *Madam Butterfly*. It is reported that she demanded—and received—three thousand dollars for each performance.

That was indeed an eventful year for it marked some of her greatest triumphs at La Scala, especially as Leonora in *Il Trovatore* and in the title rôle of *Lucia di Lammermoor* (Donizetti). Reporting her performance for the magazine *Opera*,[1] Peter Dragadze wrote:

[1] March 1954

44

MARIA MENEGHINI CALLAS

". . . . a great personal triumph, holding the public in suspense with breathtaking clarity and agility of her coloratura, which contrasted with the almost contralto quality of her voice in the recitatives and first act arias. Her 'mad scene' produced an emotional thrill that few other living singers are capable of. . . ."

One of the most interesting presentations of that season at the Scala, however, was the new production of *Alceste* (Gluck). Although it was not entirely suitable for her, Madame Callas sang the name part with great artistry, giving the same moving, expressive performance that characterised her singing of the title rôle of *La Vestale* (Spontini) which opened the following season.

An interesting eye-witness account of one of her performances at the Scala is given by Spike Hughes in his book *Great Opera Houses:*[1] "I have mentioned the purring sound which accompanies a singer of whom the Scala audience approves. There was a great deal of purring the night of *La Sonnambula* for the leading part was sung by Maria Meneghini Callas, whom the Scala public dotes on. At the end, carnations were showered on her, in ones and twos and in bunches from the topmost galleries where the spectators lean over the parapet, clinging on like monkeys at the end of the first row. It was a charming and genuine gesture which, while it is said that these demonstrations are sometimes organised by zealous husbands, nevertheless makes the English habit of having attendants bring formal baskets of flowers on to the stage a dreary impersonal gesture". One can well imagine the enthusiasm of that evening because Bellini's *La Sonnambula* contains some of the most brilliant vocal passages to be found in Italian opera, and there is not the slightest doubt that Madame Callas exploited them to the full.

By this time she was regarded as one of the greatest box-office attractions of the world's principal opera houses. She knew her value, and any impresario whose ideas did not coincide with her own on this subject was apt to find life scarcely worth living. In New York, the high fees she commanded when she was engaged for the 1956-7 season at the Metropolitan Opera House provoked a great deal of acid comment, since the principals generally receive no more than a thousand dollars for each performance. Her demands account, no doubt, for the rarity of her visits to this country, for it would appear that there is some slight restraint upon

[1] Weidenfeld & Nicholson : London 1956

45

the use of the tax-payers' money which enables Covent Garden to function.

Many of the operas in which Madame Callas appears would probably not be produced at all but for the necessity of finding works that please her and provide an effective means of displaying her voice, and the revival of trivial operas for this reason must occasionally worry a few artistic consciences. Cherubini's *Médée*, for instance, can scarcely be described as an opera of any great merit, and even *Lucia di Lammermoor*,[1] which was at one time something of a favourite in this country, is essentially a "prima donna's opera". Although it is one of Donizetti's best efforts, it has nothing of the musical or dramatic qualities of many of the more modern operas that are suffering neglect. It did, however, provide Madame Callas with another ovation when it was performed at the Vienna State Opera in 1956 under Herbert von Karajan.

Her clear, ringing tone can hold its own across a full open orchestra, and it is in many ways a pity that she has abandoned the heavier operas. Her range of expression is good, though more limited than several of the other eminent sopranos we have heard at Covent Garden in the post-war years. She can soar to tremendous heights, and it is her higher notes that often come across with the hard brilliance that we in this country associate with years of operatic work as opposed to the sweeter tones produced by some of our prominent oratorio singers. The peculiar timbre of her voice is not to everybody's liking, but it is remarkable in its flexibility and richness. Her musicianship is impeccable and she has a very real sense of drama which contributes much to her successes in opera. It would be difficult to find a soprano who could illuminate a character more vividly, or who could get a tighter grip upon the emotions of her audience. She is, in fact, typical of those who have opera in their bones; who have grown up in opera and whose whole life is dominated by this fascinating fusion of the arts.

Not all of her many recordings are available in Great Britain, but Columbia have issued a fair range which give some idea of this singer's ability, though they are anything but uniform in quality. They include several complete operas: *Norma* (conducted by Tullio Serafin 33CX1179-81), *I Puritani* (by the same conductor, 33CX1058-60), *Lucia di Lammermoor* (same conductor, 33CX1131-2), a thrilling *Cavalleria Rusticana* (same conductor, 33CXS1182-3),

---

[1] The libretto is based upon Scott's novel *The Bride of Lammermoor*

a most dramatic *Tosca* (conducted by Victor de Sabata, 33CX1094-5) and *The Force of Destiny* (conducted by Tullio Serafin, 33CX1258-60), as well as one or two opera recitals and minor items.

In private life, Maria Meneghini Callas is a rich and entertaining personality who will quickly disillusion those who imagine that the life of a prima donna is one of great leisure and ease. She studies her parts with meticulous care and spends a great deal of time in getting to understand, from the purely dramatic point of view, the character she is to impersonate. She realizes that audiences expect a thrilling performance from a prima donna, and that one or two disappointments are sufficient to make them look elsewhere.

Of her palatial house in Milan, with its imposing marble rooms and other fabulous luxuries, many stories have been told, but the writer, unfortunately, has not had an opportunity of visiting this appropriate background of one of the most fascinating personalites in the realm of opera.

Edith Coates

BORN in Lincoln of Yorkshire parents, Edith Coates is a descendant of the famous admiral Robert Blake through her mother's family: a fact of no great importance musically, but of some interest when one considers the spirit with which this well-known opera singer has climbed from the lowest rungs of the professional ladder.

At school, singing and dancing were the only subjects that appealed to her, and she had little chance of shining even in these because she was a very nervous child. Having an excellent voice she was once persuaded to sing a solo at church, but she was so terrified that she broke down in the middle of it. Not a very good start to a career in singing!

At twelve she won a scholarship to Trinity College of Music, London. Here, she tells us, Mr. Edric Cundell tried, rather unsuccessfully, to teach her the mysteries of harmony, but Mrs. Ethel Henry Bird found in her a tractable singing pupil and one who could be very useful in the opera class. She took part in several productions of Gilbert and Sullivan operas and gradually acquired a little confidence on the stage.

When she was fifteen she left Trinity College and went straight to the Old Vic to do insignificant "walking on" parts in Shakespeare, to sing an occasional song and to make herself generally useful. After three months of this she went into the chorus of the opera, and in due course was permitted to take minor solo parts. Her first, she recalls, was as the boy Lazarillo in *Maritana*, which brought down the wrath of Lilian Baylis upon her head because she wore silk stockings on the stage instead of the more appropriate worsted ones!

In those early days she first met the man who was to become her husband: Powell Lloyd. He, too, was an obscure member of the Old Vic Company—singing in the chorus and doing any odd job that came along. He was once asked to scrub out the office. So as one would imagine, these two youngsters found much in common: they shared similar trials and disappointments, the same problems

Isobel Baillie

PLATE VI

Angus McBean

Owen Brannigan

PLATE VIII

Henry Cummings

PLATE VII

EDITH COATES

and aspirations, the same financial difficulties. For singing in the chorus and doing any small part required of her, Edith Coates received the enormous salary of thirty shillings a week, and Powell Lloyd was little, if any, better off. For all that, they had a great deal of fun together: there was always something to laugh or grouse about, something to discuss with all the earnestness of youth over a cup of coffee, and the strain of touring in the provinces with twice-nightly productions of opera was borne with high-spirited fortitude.

"Nerves" were still worrying Edith Coates in those days. She remembers that once when she had but a single line to sing her heart was palpitating so violently that she could scarcely breathe!

When the reconstructed Sadler's Wells Theatre was opened, she began doing more important parts for her company (the Vic-Wells Company which later became the Sadler's Wells Opera Company when the Old Vic was used exclusively for drama). As so often happens, the opportunity of singing her first big part came quite by chance: the principal playing the part of Carmen was taken ill suddenly, and as no understudy was available, the question "Does anybody here know Carmen?" was addressed to the chorus. Edith Coates volunteered and sang the part without an orchestral rehearsal, scoring a great success.

This naturally led to her being cast for many other principal parts Delilah, Azucena (*Trovatore*), Amneris (*Aïda*), Ortrud (*Lohengrin*) and suchlike, all of which were performed without orchestral rehearsals because the company could not afford such extravagances! How much did she receive for singing these parts? Four pounds a week! Would anybody in the audience at the time have believed it?

But worse was to come. After working in this way for months, and paying out of her tiny salary fees to the various teachers to whom she went for lessons from time to time, she was called to Miss Baylis's office and informed that because she was not making the most of her opportunities she was to receive an Irishman's rise— a reduction of a pound a week in her salary! She could scarcely believe her ears.

She was so hurt that she very nearly accepted an offer made to her by the D'Oyly Carte Company, but she eventually decided to stay at "the Wells" because the D'Oyly Carte Company were about to leave England for a tour of Canada, and she did not want to leave her home in London at that time.

49

4

The following season she made a great "hit" as Lehl in *The Snow Maiden* and had the cut in her salary restored. Then she rose rapidly in the esteem of the critics, and the management made increases in her remuneration from time to time. Ultimately she received a salary of ten pounds a week which in those days seemed simply enormous to her!

By this time she was doing a small amount of concert work and building up a reputation in oratorio: she was heard in the *Messiah*, *Elijah* and other well-known works, and was particularly successful in Rossini's *Stabat Mater* and the Verdi *Requiem*. The teachers who trained her in later years were Clive Carey, Esta D'Argo, Dino Borgioli and Dawson Freer.

When in 1937 *Hänsel and Gretel* was produced at Covent Garden under the direction of Sir Thomas Beecham, the singer engaged for the part of the children's mother was taken ill, and at the last moment, Edith Coates, who was singing the part at Sadler's Wells at the time, was asked to take her place. Unfortunately, the Covent Garden production was in German while at "the Wells" it was being sung in English. Miss Coates could not of course learn the German text in an hour or so, consequently she was obliged to sing it in English, and Sir Thomas had to apologise to the audience for the mixture of languages, explaining in his own inimitable way that at very short notice they had been obliged to get a substitute from "another institution".

Miss Coates's success in this production led to her being chosen to take part in the magnificent performance of *The Ring* under Dr. Furtwängler later that year in the Coronation Season. In this she again distinguished herself, and was re-engaged for the two following seasons; the last before the war years, when to our national shame, the great opera house was used as a dance hall.

During the war, Miss Coates made several prolonged tours with the Sadler's Wells Opera Company, chiefly in the provinces. At Hull she had a very narrow escape while staying in the centre of the town, for in a severe air-raid almost every building around her was destroyed or set alight.

One of her greatest wartime successes was as Lucy Lockit in *The Beggar's Opera* at the New Theatre, though there were also some highly complimentary comments about her impersonation of Rosina in *The Barber of Seville*.

EDITH COATES

After the war she resigned her regular appointment with the Sadler's Wells Company but continued to work with them as a guest artist from time to time, as for instance in 1945, when she played in their first production of *Peter Grimes*. She also went with them on their tour of Germany, playing in most of the principal cities.

Edith Coates joined the Covent Garden Company in 1947 and in such operas as *Carmen, Il Trovatore, Rigoletto* and *Peter Grimes* soon became a favourite with those who patronize our principal opera house. Her greatest audiences, of course, are the millions who listen to broadcast opera, for she has taken part in many studio productions, notably *Aïda* and *Schwanda the Bagpiper*.

In the years 1949-1954 she sang in several cycles of *The Ring* with Flagstad, Hotter and Svanholm, her Waltraute in *Götterdämmerung* being particularly brilliant. In *The Year's Work in Music*, Philip Hope-Wallace described it as a success that not even Madame Flagstad's Brünnhilde could overshadow. In Coronation Year (1953) she also sang the part of the Queen of the Gypsies in Sir Thomas Beecham's revival of Balfe's opera *The Bohemian Girl*, and took part with Kirsten Flagstad in the production of *Dido and Aeneas* at the Mermaid Theatre in St. John's Wood.

Subsequently, she has returned to Sadler's Wells as guest artist in Janáček's delightful opera *Katya Kabanova* (1954, under the direction of Rafael Kubelik) and for the first English performance of *Jenufa*, by the same composer, in 1956.

It has also given her great pleasure to sing in first performances of several English operas, *The Olympians* (Sir Arthur Bliss), *The Midsummer Marriage* (Michael Tippett), for instance, at Covent Garden; and at the Minack Open Air Theatre in Cornwall the première of Inglis Gundry's Cornish opera *The Logan Rock*.

Three operas in which she has, in recent years, achieved outstanding successes are *Elektra* (Strauss), in which she played Clytemnestra, Berg's *Wozzeck*, and *The Queen of Spades* (Tchaikovsky). In these she gratefully acknowledges the help given to her by the late Erich Kleiber in achieving those striking musical characterisations that were so warmly praised by the leading critics.

Incidentally, she appeared in the first opera to be specially commissioned for television in this country: Arthur Benjamin's *Mañana*, and also sang in the film that Sir Laurence Olivier made of *The Beggar's Opera*.

To those who wish to make a career in opera, Miss Coates has no hesitation in saying that the best way is to start at the bottom and work one's way up through the chorus, because by this method one assimilates the art of the theatre gradually and gains confidence at the same time. Singers who are suddenly transplanted, as it where, from the concert hall into the opera house seldom reach perfection by modern standards for they lack the dramatic training which is so essential.

The modern tendency is towards more dramatic opera, which is just as it should be, for opera is a fusion of many arts. In the old days when opera was little more than a concert performance in costume with a small amount of action, a singer with a good voice but no dramatic training could generally " get away with it ", but now the art has progressed and dramatic merit is demanded. One of the most important things an opera singer has to remember nowadays is to keep his acting and singing balanced, so that it is a unified art-form. One so often finds a singer neglecting his movements when he has something exacting to sing, or conversely, scamping his singing because he is so engrossed in his acting. A principal who has had a few years in the chorus is less likely to do this because he has probably got the theatre "into his bones". For the same reason, experience in the acting of plays is always of value to those aspiring to principal parts in opera, and Miss Coates also believes that training in dancing—particularly ballet—is helpful to *any* opera singer.

Many singers try to get into opera when their voices are entirely unsuited to it. A "cold" voice is of very little use—there are but one or two rôles in which it could be employed. It is therefore essential that aspirants should be able to produce a variety of tone colours, and if they are in any doubt about their ability to do so they should consult a teacher experienced in this specialized branch of singing, even before they enter the chorus.

At the present time there are fairly frequent opportunities of joining a chorus, because in London there are two full-time opera companies (Covent Garden and Sadler's Wells), both of which offer splendid training; then there is also the Carl Rosa Company which employs a substantial chorus. This company now spends most of its time on tour.

It should always be borne in mind that opera singing is a great strain physically, mentally and vocally. A strong "natural" voice is of course the first essential: a voice lacking power is useless, especially in the music-dramas of Wagner when they are performed with an open orchestra (i.e., an orchestra playing in a pit that is not covered or hooded). Few people realize the strain of singing across a large orchestra for a whole evening: the operas of Strauss, particularly, are very tiring. Therefore the singer must use his voice with some restraint, relying upon clear articulation to get the words over. It might be said here that in order to avoid tiring the voice, Miss Coates makes a practice of talking as little as possible before an opera, or during the performance when she is off the stage. She also likes to take a short walk before the evening performance to get a breath of fresh air.

Her chief criticism of the younger singers of today is their lack of good articulation, which, she says, is a thing that cannot be overdone in opera. She also feels that some of them try to master too many rôles at once: they would do better to specialize for a year or two in just a couple of parts exactly suited to their voices. They should also try to get experience abroad, if possible. Miss Coates believes that such experience would have helped her enormously in her early days.

The difficulty of getting adequate training probably accounts for the scarcity of really good young sopranos and contraltos at the present time. Miss Coates feels that there is too much casual treatment of our more promising young artists: in other countries far greater efforts would be made to give them the sort of training they deserve.

Her own voice is one of special interest because when she first went to Sadler's Wells she possessed only a very limited contralto compass, but the range gradually increased—although she made no special effort to extend her voice—and she now has well over two-and-a-half octaves: she can sing a substantial bottom E and reach a top C with ease. Few mezzo-soprano rôles are too high for her.

Miss Coates never worries about registers, and she believes that it is very foolish to imitate the old Italian mezzo-sopranos who used to "change gear" quite deliberately when passing from the higher to the lower registers, or vice versa. She dislikes the "gallon-jar" type of contralto. Like Caruso, she finds that a glass of sherry before singing can be beneficial, but she would hesitate to recommend that famous singer's other habits: the smoking of a cigar, the eating of an apple or drinking of brandy before a performance!

Her preferences in opera are for the works of Verdi and Wagner. She loves rôles that are really dramatic, and that perhaps explains why she deplores the unwarrantable neglect of Dame Ethel Smyth's splendid opera *The Wreckers*. It will be a long time before she forgets the thrill she experienced when playing in it at Sadler's Wells, in the presence of the composer, just before the war.

A generous warm-hearted personality, Edith Coates is well known in the theatre world for her high spirits and sense of humour: it is said that she can laugh anything off. She loves parties and gay company, going to the theatre (she is deeply appreciative of Shakespeare) and to the cinema, particularly if a French film is being exhibited. Yet at home she is quite domesticated, and enjoys doing a little housework as a change from singing. A casual caller in wintertime would probably find her sitting beside the fire with her husband, nursing the cat and listening to the wireless; plays being as popular with her as broadcasts of music. Her reading is chiefly of biography, history, thrillers—and Dickens.

Powell Lloyd, whom she married in 1933, stayed in opera for many years but frequently digressed into Shakespeare, and several times before the war he had the honour of playing beside John Gielgud. He has also done excellent work as a producer and scenic designer, and at the present time is doing this type of work as a free lance.

Joan Cross

JOAN CROSS was "born with a love of the theatre", to use her
own words, and if she had not been given a good singing voice and
a musical education she would probably have distinguished herself
in drama as readily as she has made her name as an opera singer.

She is a Londoner, born at the beginning of the century. Her
mother, who had a passion for the violin, hopefully presented her
with a small fiddle when she was six, and Joan was soon scraping
out an occasional obbligato to the songs her mother sang at parties.
But it was not until she went to St. Paul's Girls' School at the age of
twelve that she came into contact with "serious music". She was
quite enthralled, for Gustav Holst was the music master there and
inspired everybody with a deep and serious love of the art. His
enthusiasm and intense musicianship made a deep impression upon
her, and it was with great joy that she played in the school orchestra,
eventually achieving the concert platform when she was called upon
to play at Speech Day celebrations.

A scholarship for the violin then took her to Trinity College of
Music, London, where for a while she studied with the eminent
French violinist Emile Sauret. Alas! he displayed no great enthusiasm for her talents, and she realized that they were insufficient for
a career as a solo violinist. She had, rather casually, taken singing
as her second subject, and as her voice showed signs of development
she asked her singing teacher what chances it had of improvement.
But she was assured that it could be nothing more than a "pretty
drawing-room voice". She went home very crestfallen, but after
thinking it over decided to get a second opinion. She went to
another teacher and to her great joy was told that she stood quite
a good chance of doing something in the world of song, so she went
to Dr. Charles Pearce, the Principal of Trinity College at that time,
and asked for permission to concentrate upon singing instead of the
violin. He agreed, and she became a pupil of Dawson Freer, whose
expert knowledge was to guide her for many years.

Joan Cross made such good progress as a singing student that her

55

scholarship was extended considerably, and when eventually she left the College she was given a letter of recommendation to Lilian Baylis at the Old Vic. How vividly she remembers the audition. Horribly nervous, she walked on to the stage, sang Nedda's song from *Pagliacci* as if she had been standing on the platform of a parish hall, and walked off again. Miss Baylis then called her back and told her that she couldn't offer her a job but if she wished she could work in the chorus for nothing to gain experience!

Excited and bewildered, Joan left the theatre feeling that a tremendous honour had been conferred upon her! She had never met anybody so terrifying as the brusque Lilian Baylis, and she little realized the great influence that this remarkable woman was soon to exert upon her life. Joan feared, loved and occasionally laughed at her, but at the same time grew to admire her whole-heartedly, and was inspired by her to concentrate all her efforts in a single-minded and sincere ambition to better the cause of opera in English. Like many other singers, musicians and players of Miss Baylis's time, Joan Cross developed a real passion for the Old Vic and Sadler's Wells.

Lilian Baylis told her bluntly that she had a voice but couldn't act, and gave her permission to watch the rehearsals and perform-ances of the Shakespeare plays so that she could pick up something of the art. This meant that Joan had the freedom of the theatre, and nothing could have delighted her more, for she was burning with stage fever and it was a thrill even to run an errand for one of the talented young actors that were making a name in that historic old theatre. There were only two opera productions a week, the rest of the time being taken up by the dramatic performances, but Joan simply lived in the theatre from Monday morning to Saturday night. It was, she says, an existence of "sheer joy and magic". In opera she sang in the chorus and played a few minor parts —and that meant singing in anything from *Maritana* to the great music-dramas of Wagner—and because she was always on the spot she was fre-quently given the chance of playing little parts in some of the Shakespearian productions for which the Old Vic was famous. She still recalls how in the masque in Robert Atkins' production of *The Tempest* she had to make her entry by walking over some "rocks" at the back of the stage. At the dress rehearsal she was being very careful not to trip as she descended when suddenly Atkins bellowed at her: "Don't look at your feet!"

56

JOAN CROSS

In those days of youthful enthusiasm, the theatre became almost an obsession. She would leave her home in Essex early in the morning, travel to Charing Cross by the District Railway, cross Hungerford Bridge and simply tear along Waterloo Road in her anxiety to get to the Old Vic as quickly as possible. Even when the theatre was closed in the summer she still made the journey across the river to make quite sure that the beloved opera-house was still there! If there was nothing much for her to do she would watch the rehearsals, talk to the scene-shifters, and even go up to the "wardrobe" to watch the costumes being made. She existed chiefly on coffee and buns bought at the "Pearce and Plenty" café, which in those days occupied the site on which the box office was later built. How she idolized such actors as Ion Swinley, George Hayes and David Hay Petrie! The last-named, a wonderful Shakespearian clown, was her "ideal" in those days.

Even in later years, when she was playing principal parts, Joan attended the Shakespeare rehearsals, especially if John Gielgud happened to be in the cast! She saw *Richard II* over twenty times from various parts of the theatre. After days spent in this manner she would return to Charing Cross somewhere around eleven o'clock at night and catch a train home to bed and dreams of the theatre!

One of her greatest friends at the Old Vic was the late Charles Corri, the director of music: a remarkable character lacking in personal gloss but one of the soundest musicians one could wish to meet. He was a typical Londoner and, having acquired his art in the hard school of practical experience, never minced his words, but he was kindness itself to those who took no offence at his brusque manner. For all engaged in the Old Vic operas it was a case of "sink or swim": there was but one rehearsal for each performance, and newcomers lived in a perpetual state of anxiety. No one could have done more than Corri to keep everything together, and by realizing this Joan Cross won his favour. But that did not exempt her from receiving a sharp word of censure from time to time! She will never forget the performance of *Tannhäuser* in which, during the Venusberg music, she somehow missed a bar. In a loud and trucculent voice he snapped to the leader of the orchestra: "She's a bar ahead, the bitch."

At the end of her first season Joan Cross felt that she had become a moderately useful member of the company, and was affronted when Lilian Baylis still refused to pay her a salary. She appreciated Miss Baylis's acute financial difficulties but had her own problems, too, for her family were thinking it was high time that she began to earn her own living. So with a very heavy heart she left the Old Vic and spent the next few months in taking minor concert engagements.

Without the excitement of the theatre, life seemed very dull, and it was a tremendous joy to her when one day she received from Lilian Baylis a letter inviting her to return and play the part of Cherubino in *Figaro*. Her outstanding success in this rôle secured her permanent membership of the company, and in the years to come she was to play nearly fifty important parts. One of her earliest "hits" was as Elizabeth in *Tannhäuser*.

Joan Cross played continuously at the Old Vic and Sadler's Wells (which became the home of the opera company when the Old Vic was given over entirely to drama) from 1926 to 1939. Her experiences would fill a book—and probably will if she can ever be persuaded to write an autobiography. The many thousands who have patronized those historic theatres will recall with pleasure her fine impersonations of such characters as the Countess in *Figaro*, Pamina in *The Magic Flute*, Desdemona in *Othello*, Sieglinde in *The Valkyrie*, Elsa in *Lohengrin*, Marschallin in Strauss's *Rosenkavalier* (which she has recently produced for Covent Garden) and, of course, as Madam Butterfly.

One of her most vivid memories is of an absent-minded stage manager they had at one time. To the astonishment of all concerned he once lowered the curtain in the middle of a dramatic scene in *Madam Butterfly* and the company performed for a minute or two out of sight of the audience. To make up for this he raised the curtain on another occasion while the scenes were being shifted, much to the horror of various members of the company who were sitting about on the stage in most undignified attitudes.

Joan Cross admits that she has often sung parts outside her normal vocal range—parts for which she would not have been cast in other opera houses, but is grateful for the opportunities of doing such things under the comparatively easier conditions that prevailed at the Old Vic. She criticizes herself for having accepted these parts, and acknowledges that she was "mad" to sing, as she did on one occasion, *The Magic Flute* at a Saturday matinee at the

Old Vic and on the same day an evening performance of *Bohème* at Covent Garden. She also recalls singing in a matinee performance of *Othello* and, owing to the sudden illness of a fellow artist, in *Figaro* the same evening. She sang in *Othello* at Covent Garden and says that she did not meet the tenor until the actual performance, a state of affairs that was grossly unfair to any young performer.

In passing, it should be recorded that Miss Cross had the honour of singing in the first English performance of *The Bartered Bride*. This was the Oxford University Opera Club's production in 1929.

When in 1940 the heavy air-raids brought the work of Sadler's Wells to a standstill, Joan Cross was one of the small company of about a dozen singers that Tyrone Guthrie formed to take opera into the provinces. Their enterprise was deeply appreciated in all the places they visited, and in due course it was possible to add to their numbers and play in the "No. 1 towns". It was then that Joan Cross was asked to undertake the arduous task of director, and she soon discovered that the difficulties of the job were greatly aggravated by wartime conditions and shortages. The work went on week after week despite the irksome conditions: wearisome travelling, wretched lodgings, air-raids that seemed to come just when human endurance was at its weakest, severely limited finances, shortages of wood and canvas, and so forth. Yet it was by carrying on the good work in the provinces that they were able to give London seasons at the New Theatre, which became their wartime home when "the Wells" was temporarily put out of use.

Perhaps the greatest of all their wartime achievements was the first production of *Peter Grimes* in February 1944. Benjamin Britten had played his score to Joan Cross and Lawrance Collingwood in Liverpool and they had at once persuaded Tyrone Guthrie to put the new opera into production despite the great risk of attempting to mount an entirely new work in wartime. This extremely original opera provoked a great deal of antagonism but it succeeded, nevertheless, and won a permanent place in the Sadler's Wells repertoire. In the original production Joan Cross played the part of Ellen Orford. Another of Benjamin Britten's operas in which she has distinguished herself is *The Turn of the Screw*, of which a longplaying recording has been made by Decca (LXT 5038-9).

Before she resigned from Sadler's Wells in 1945 she had the pleasure of seeing it re-opened with a company at almost full strength; a company that had for several years paid its way—an unheard-of achievement in the realm of opera. Since then she has associated herself with the English Opera Group, a small body of young people who gathered to present English opera in such a way that it could be given in smaller theatres and to encourage those young composers and poets who, having written for the opera house, were faced with seemingly-insuperable difficulties in getting their work produced.

In recent years, Miss Cross, whose achievements have earned her the C.B.E., has fulfilled another of her dearest ambitions: the establishment of an opera school where young singers can receive "the part of their training that is not available elsewhere". Here she is trying to make it possible for operatic aspirants to enjoy some of the privileges that she received at the Old Vic in those wonderful days of the Lilian Baylis régime, principally in connection with the dramatic side of the opera singer's work.

Henry Cummings

IN Henry Cummings we have a baritone who is endeavouring to carry on the great traditions of Robert Radford, Joan Coates and Plunket Greene. Few English singers are better equipped to do so, for he was in turn a pupil of all three of them, and not a word of their wisdom was wasted upon him. He is the type of singer who takes his art very seriously, who is content to spend the whole of his life in seeking perfection, knowing full well that he will probably never be wholly satisfied with his efforts. In short, he is an artist.

He was born in Dublin in 1906 of a Scottish father and a Staffordshire mother, and at the age of eight weeks was taken to Watford, where all the early part of his life was spent. When he was four he contracted infantile paralysis, and for the next three years was completely crippled; indeed, he was given up as a hopeless case. Much of his childhood was spent in Guy's Hospital, and he had to endure many operations, but he never lost heart, and gradually some improvement was made. A normal education was of course impossible, but he was well served by private tutors and was an unusually intelligent lad.

His voice broke when he was about fifteen. Evidently it was quite a sudden process with him for he distinctly remembers that after four days of speaking in a "cracked" voice he was accepted as a bass singer in the choir of St. Michael-and-All-Angels, Watford; a church noted for its fine music.

Deciding to make music his career, he went to the Watford School of Music and studied for three-and-a-half years. Then after a few years with Gilbert Bailey he went to Norman Allin for advice, and this eminent singer recommended that he should study with Robert Radford at the Royal Academy of Music. This he did, and at the end of his first three months there won the Mario Prize. Later, he received the Burgess Grant and the Westmorland Scholarship, and ultimately became an Associate.

He stayed with Radford until that famous opera and oratorio singer died in 1933. Then John Coates (1865-1941) accepted him as a pupil for a while, and finally, he studied with Plunket Greene.

But we are proceeding too quickly, and if this sketch is to have any chronological order at all we must retrace out steps and return to Cummings's student days, for he was still at the Academy when he was "discovered" by the BBC. He was singing at a students' concert in the Queen's Hall under Sir Henry J. Wood, at which a talented fellow-student, Florence Hooton, was playing the 'cello. Representatives of the BBC were present, and were impressed by both soloists, so the two students received their first broadcasting engagements at about the same time. Both became regular broadcasters, and Henry Cummings has now been "on the air" well over four hundred times.

His career then developed on much the same lines as other English singers: a great deal of oratorio work all over the British Isles, and other interesting engagements from time to time both in this country and in Holland (where he sang the part of Amfortas in *Parsifal* in 1939 and appeared as soloist in two performances of Walton's magnificent oratorio *Belshazzar's Feast* in 1946); many recitals, promenade concerts, and so forth. But a word should be said about one or two of his specialities, such as the songs of Liszt, of which he is perhaps this country's leading exponent, other lieder and the songs of certain British composers. His favourite works include the Bach *St. Matthew Passion*, the Beethoven Choral Symphony, the *Requiem* of Brahms, Handel's *Acis and Galatea*, Haydn's *Creation* (which he regards as one of the finest oratorios we possess) the *Requiem* of Verdi, Elgar's *Dream of Gerontius* and *The Apostles*, Hamilton Harty's *Mystic Trumpeter* (a work unjustifiably neglected) and Stanford's *Songs of the Sea* and *Songs of the Fleet*.

Cummings has had the honour of singing in the first performance of many works by contemporary composers, and he recalls with special pleasure his part in Leslie Woodgate's oratorio *Simon Peter* with the Leicester Philharmonic Society under the composer's baton.

He has sung in most of the big musical festivals and for practically all the famous societies, and has many happy memories of them. Somewhat less happy, but amusing nevertheless, is his recollection of one of the minor festivals, at which he sang in *Elijah* under a famous visiting conductor. The orchestra lost their heads completely in *Is not His word like a fire?* and Cummings came to the end of the aria accompanied by a single string bass, with the conductor still maintaining a steady beat but with an expression of exasperated resignation upon his face.

To those aspiring to successful careers as singers, Henry Cummings declares: "There is no short cut to fame in singing. Beware of fancy 'systems', avoid the 'methods' of quacks who promise an easy road to success. A singer must first of all possess a voice fit to be trained, and then be prepared to spend many years in developing it. Only by going through the 'bitter grind' can one hope to become a true musician."

He fully endorses Plunket Greene's statement that "98 per cent of singing is breath control". This is the secret—the beginning and the end of singing.

Cummings does not agree with those who say that the days of great singing have passed. People are still being born with lovely voices, but it is the shortage of great teachers that is responsible for the so-called decline in singing. The fully-fledged concert or opera singer needs a teacher as much as the student, since it is only by singing occasionally to a responsible fellow-singer or teacher and seeking his candid criticism, that he can keep himself in good form and eradicate all those bad habits that every singer is apt to acquire. It is so easy to drop into such habits.

At heart, Henry Cummings is a countryman, and although his work entails much travel as well as prolonged visits to London and provincial centres he loves to return to his Dorset home—not far from Bournemouth—and there to spend hours doing odd jobs in his garden. See him in his shirt-sleeves felling a tree and you find it hard to believe that he spent his boyhood in fighting one of the worst diseases that can assail the human form. He has one very peculiar hobby—for a musician, anyway—the breeding of tropical fish. His various aquaria contain many fine specimens.

He was married in 1934 to Kathleen Stanley Jones, and has three daughters: Jane Elizabeth, Susan Catherin, and Hannah Mary. The two elder children are enthusiastic 'cellists, both of them having taken to their instruments without a word of parental persuasion.

Astra Desmond

HALF a century or more ago professional singers were regarded as rather worse than solo violinists for their extremely limited knowledge of music and general illiteracy. There were some honourable exceptions, of course, but one-track minds were the rule, and this popular notion was not unjustified. Nowadays, most audiences—but not all—demand something more than a beautiful voice, and soloists are expected to have at least a sound general knowledge of music. In the case of Astra Desmond we have a singer whose mental equipment is far above the average: she possesses a B.A. Honours degree in Classics, can speak nearly a dozen languages, and is able to undertake research into the music of any European nation. We hear her rarely in the concert hall nowadays because she is devoting all her time to her work as a professor of singing at the Royal Academy of Music, but it will be a long time before her singing is forgotten, especially by those fortunate students who are now deriving the benefit of her wide experience.

She is a native of Torquay. In her early days at home she was the alto and accompanist of a quartet made up of her sister (soprano), father (tenor) and her brother (baritone), a modest little ensemble whose aspirations rarely rose above Gilbert and Sullivan!

In all educational subjects Astra Desmond was a precocious child, and while she was at the Notting Hill High School she won the first of a series of scholarships that enabled her to keep and educate herself for many years after. This is important, because contrary to a supposition that is widely held in musical circles, she had no "silver spoon": her parents were of very limited means.

She was about seventeen when she won the Westfield College Classical Scholarship. Her original intention was to study medicine, but a strong love of the classics prevailed, and she took her degree as a specialist in Latin and Greek when she was about twenty.

Because her mother was at that time in Australia, she planned to take a lectureship there, but a member of the college staff urged her to consider a singing career, for her contribution to college

Baron

Elisabeth Schwarzkopf as Susanna in *The Marriage of Figaro*

PLATE IX

Swarbrick Studios

Edith Coates

PLATE X

Ibbs & Tillett

Astra Desmond, C.B.E.

PLATE XI

Joan Cross

PLATE XII

concerts had impressed many discriminating people who felt that her voice had great possibilities. It was this that made her go to Blanche Marchesi for advice. The famous singer was convinced that her voice was worth training, but Miss Desmond still hesitated because she had not the means to keep herself for any length of time. Fortunately, the Mary South Scholarship was then announced, and she not only won this award (which provided the funds for the recipient to study with Madame Marchesi) but obtained a maintenance grant as well.

Miss Desmond spent four years with Madame Marchesi, during which she made many successful appearances in the concert hall and opera house. She even accepted a permanent appointment with the Carl Rosa Opera Company, but after a while the strain of fulfilling this undertaking before her voice was fully trained became too great, and her health gave out. She realizes now how foolish it was to accept such a post while she was still in training, and advises promising young singers of today not to make the same mistake. It was also in those early days that she was first engaged for the Boosey Ballad Concerts: a remarkable series in which she sang for many years.

In 1920 Miss Desmond married Thomas Neame, a prominent Kent agriculturist, and in the same year made her first appearance at a Three Choirs Festival, thus commencing her long association with Sir Edward Elgar. On that occasion she was the soloist in his cantata *The Music Makers*, and in the next few years she appeared as contralto soloist in most of his other works. She has many treasured memories of that great composer, who was a good friend both to her and her husband. He was always very particular about the attire of his soloists, and Miss Desmond recalls how he would come to her before every performance with the words: "Now let me see what you're wearing!"

During one of the festivals Elgar stayed at the same hotel as Astra Desmond and her husband, so they invariably had meals at the same table. One morning at breakfast Sir Edward looked up from his paper and asked Miss Desmond to put her leg out, much to everybody's surprise. Nevertheless, she obliged. "No good!" the composer declared, and then to satisfy everyone's curiosity he explained that there was a horse called "Grey Silk Stockings" running that day and if Miss Desmond had been wearing stockings of that colour he would have backed it.

5

Miss Desmond's authoritative interpretations of everything Elgar wrote for the contralto voice are far famed—as the Angel in *The Dream of Gerontius*, for instance, she has few equals—and she is justly proud to be able to claim that in the last year of Elgar's life she sang all his major works under his own direction. Her reading of the part of Mary Magdalene in *The Apostles* has, as the *Musical Times* once said, a touch of genius.

Although much of her time has been taken up in attendance at the greater musical festivals at home and abroad, she has made many welcome returns to the opera house. In such rôles as Ortrud, Carmen, Amneris and Delilah, she has often distinguished herself, and she is proud to have taken part in two productions of operas by our own Rutland Boughton: in *Alkestis* in that composer's brave but ill-fated enterprise at Glastonbury, and in the production of *The Ever Young* at Bath. It is also worth recording that she went to Paris to take a leading part in Stravinsky's *Oedipus Rex* under the composer's direction. Stravinsky was so engrossed in making a success of his opera that he gave no thought whatever to the strain on the voice of his soloists at the seemingly endless rehearsals, and Miss Desmond can recall no other occasion in her career when her voice has been used so ruthlessly. This, however, does not affect her estimation of Stravinsky as a composer.

Much could be written about her tours abroad. She has sung with great success in Italy, Holland, Greece and the Balkans, Scandinavia, America, Spain, Portugal and France, and her great linguistic gifts have enabled her to sing the songs of about a dozen countries in their original languages. When she visited Scotland in 1944 to sing to some Norwegian troops stationed there, she took a selection of their own songs. These she sang in their native tongue so convincingly that nobody would believe that she was English. Perhaps it should be said here that she had made a special study of Scandinavian music some years previously and been decorated for her efforts by the King of Norway, from whom she received the Medal of St. Olav. She is recognized in many countries as an authority on the songs of Grieg, Sibelius and Dvořák. During the Grieg centenary celebrations held in London in 1943 Miss Desmond gave a recital of that composer's songs before the King of Norway and the Crown Prince.

In 1940 she went to Greece to give five concerts, one of them

66

with the Royal Hellenic Orchestra before the late King, and after the war she made a return visit to that country under the auspices of the British Council and the Army Welfare authorities. Another interesting journey made at the request of the British Council was to Portugal in 1941, when she gave a memorable recital including some Portuguese songs in Lisbon. On the day the Second World War finished she was in Brussels with Gerald Moore on yet another recital tour.

Astra Desmond was appointed to a professorship at the Royal Academy of Music in 1946. It should also be mentioned that in 1950 she became the first woman President of the Incorporated Society of Musicians, and that from 1952 to 1956 she was President of the Society of Women Musicians. She is a member of the Advisory Panel of the Arts Council, of the Musical Advisory Committee of the BBC, and of the Governing Council of the Carl Rosa Opera Trust. She was awarded the C.B.E. in the 1949 New Year's Honours List.

She believes that in England today there are some of the finest voices in the world, but we have two deficiencies: the serious shortage of good teachers and the lack of opera centres in the provinces. Because of the latter, the younger singers of today have so few opportunities to climb to eminence. If we had thriving provincial opera houses, as in certain countries abroad, young singers would have both the opportunity and encouragement to perfect their technique, as well as the prospect of a secure and permanent career. We should then have really well-trained young singers coming to London. As it is, the necessity for good technique is often disregarded, since it is possible for a young man or woman blessed with a fine voice to make a "hit" in London with very little technique.

Conditions in this country today tend to encourage young singers to go on the platform before they know their job. However perfect and beautiful their voices may be, they should be taught to understand the vocal art: to know precisely *why* their singing is good because the day would come when they would have to sing against their inclination, under the stress of illness or other adverse conditions. Then they would get into difficulties if they had no real technique.

It is essential that every singer should understand the principles of scientific breathing. This is of course a matter that cannot be discussed briefly, but Miss Desmond recommends *daily* breathing exercises for all beginners together with a few physical exercises for the development of the abdominal muscles, in addition to their normal daily singing practice.

Miss Desmond considers that most singers need only a few basic exercises to keep the voice in good form, and she recommends that these should be sufficiently simple to be memorized, so that the attention can be concentrated entirely upon voice production. She agrees with most other teachers that short periods of regular practice are far more effective than long periods at irregular intervals.

It is not generally realized how many singers spoil their voices by attempting the wrong sort of repertoire, and Miss Desmond observes that this is not merely a matter of range. Too many light singers endanger their voices by attempting heavy rôles.

Astra Desmond undoubtedly possesses one of the finest contralto voices in England today. It is warm and colourful, exquisitely produced, and lacks that "gallon jar" quality that contraltos so often acquire. It is even and steady throughout its very considerable compass and always seems to be perfectly flexible. Her diction is above reproach.

To give details of even major items in her vast repertoire would be impossible here, but a word should be said about her fine recordings of several delightful songs of Purcell for Decca, including *Mad Bess, Celia has a thousand charms,* the *Evening Hymn, From rosy bow'rs, Hark the echoing air,* and the ever-popular *Nymphs and Shepherds.* For the same company she has also recorded the Schumann *Frauenliebe und Leben* Opus 42.

She follows the works of our contemporary composers with interest, and has the greatest admiration for many of them, especially William Walton and Dr. R. Vaughan Williams, whose *Five Tudor Portraits* have provided her with one of her most successful rôles: Drunken Alice, in which she balances upon the fine line that divides comedy from vulgarity. And while the subject of her repertoire is being mentioned, it should be stated that she introduced the songs of Yriö Kilpinen, the Finnish composer, to this country.

Miss Desmond's principal recreation is the study of languages, which is the outcome of her insatiable passion for discovering new songs, as she heartily dislikes singing translations, and if a new and appealing song is discovered among the works of a composer whose language she does not understand she sets about learning that tongue forthwith! What will happen when some enterprising young Chinese composer sends her something we do not know.

In her general reading she favours enlightened works on religion; for she heartily agrees with certain other biographees in this volume who maintain that only a return to the principles of Christianity can save the world from the disaster that threatens all people at the present time.

Life on her husband's extensive farm in Kent provides a welcome contrast to the confines of her London flat and the tension of a busy career in music. She takes a keen interest in things agricultural, but admits that when there is work to be done she rarely goes further than the garden! A reasonable amount of "mild" gardening, however, is more agreeable to her than domestic work, which she positively loathes. She has three sons.

Robert Easton

ANOTHER of the richer personalities in singing today is Robert Easton: a fine bass who has grown as an artist with every year of experience he has enjoyed. This, unfortunately, cannot be said about all the singers of his generation, for when they pass their fortieth birthday so many of those blessed with a good voice rest upon the merits of it and settle down to a comfortable "middle age" of well-paid mediocrity.

Easton was born in Sunderland and sang in a church choir from the age of six. He left school at seventeen and went straight into the army, for the Great War was then in progress. Severely wounded, he was taken to hospital and detained for three-and-a-half years, during which time he had plenty of opportunity to ponder upon his future and the problems of making a living with the disability of an artificial leg. Having done a fair amount of singing as an amateur he was keen to take up the art professionally, and was encouraged in this by the commandant of the hospital.

So when he returned home, Easton began building up a career in song by accepting all manner of modest engagements: invitations to sing at Masonic dinners, National Sunday League Concerts, and suchlike. He had lessons first from an Italian teacher named Bozzelli, then he went to Plunket Greene and Dinh Gilly, the operatic baritone.

An outstanding success at the British Empire Festival at the Albert Hall in 1922 brought a substantial increase in the amount of work offered to him, but it was not until 1926 that he was invited to make his first appearance at a promenade concert. Since then he has been a regular soloist in the promenade seasons.

His first opportunity to sing at what one might call a first-class musical event came in 1929 when he deputized for Harold Williams at a Crystal Palace performance of the *Messiah* under Sir Thomas Beecham, and this led to a great deal more work of the same kind, including engagements with the leading choral societies and at all the musical festivals with the exception of the Three Choirs.

ROBERT EASTON

In 1933 he made his début in opera at Covent Garden. His first season at the Royal Opera House gave him a chance to gain experience in minor rôles, but in the five following years he was able to take more important parts with leading Italian and German artists, notably in *Rigoletto*, *Louise*, *Parsifal* and *La Bohème*. He discovered that the Italian approach to opera was essentially individualistic (nothing mattered so long as the principals did well) whereas the Germans always believed in team-work (everybody in the cast making a significant contribution to the work as a whole), and consequently the latter were far more helpful to the English singers.

Thus Robert Easton was at Covent Garden until 1939 and at the same time was able to establish for himself an excellent reputation as an oratorio singer. He had the honour of singing in the Westminster Abbey choir at the Coronation of the late King and Queen, and was one of the soloists at the Command Performance and the Jubilee of the late Sir Henry Wood in 1937. Three years later he gave a special recital to Queen Mary and in June of the same year—1940—narrowly escaped being captured by the Germans while singing to our troops in France.

The works of Handel occupy a prominent place in Easton's large repertoire: he finds them so satisfying vocally and considers that they afford splendid exercise for the voice. Incidentally, he believes that singers aspiring to fame in opera should first have a thorough grounding in oratorio, because in opera the singer is tempted to allow his emotions to run away with his technique. There is of course less danger of this happening in oratorio.

His own voice is of excellent quality and possesses a range of over two-and-a-half octaves, from B-flat to F-sharp. Much of his success is probably due to the fact that he has always borne in mind Plunket Greene's insistence on bringing out the poetry of the song; the voice being only part of the presentation. He also believes that the possession of a sense of humour is an attribute essential to a good singer: it can have a marked effect upon one's interpretative powers. And in passing, it might be said that Easton can think of no other profession he would have enjoyed so much as singing, chiefly because of the friendliness and co-operation he has enjoyed from his brother and sister artists.

In recent years, while continuing to hold his enviable engagements as a soloist for some of our principal choral societies, he has also undertaken some interesting work in arranging programmes of songs for the BBC, and adjudicating at a variety of musical festivals up and down the country.

To the rising bass singer of today he would say that one of the most important things to remember is to avoid woolliness of tone, and he believes that this can best be done by making full use of the head resonance and avoiding distortion of the vowels.

Many amateurs are also devoting so much of their attention to the production of good tone that they are overlooking the importance of being able to produce a well-varied range of tone-colours, which is one of the fundamentals of good interpretation.

Although fatigue will often cause people to sing flat and nervousness will sometimes make them get sharp, Easton believes that out-of-tune singing is more often the result of lack of concentration, not only of mind but of the delivery of the voice, which at all times must be directed properly.

Unlike many of our leading singers, Easton does not adopt a hostile attitude towards crooners, for although he would hesitate to class them as singers, he thinks that many vocalists could learn something from these much-abused entertainers: their apparent sincerity and their success in conveying both the message and mood of their songs. They may be purveyors of sickly sentimentality, and their efforts are probably overdone, but they *do* succeed in their purpose, which is more than one can say about some of our present-day vocalists who sing about love as if they were talking about stewed steak and carrots!

Similarly, Easton is tolerant towards the more popular type of music and frequently sings songs that would provoke sneers from the pseudo-intellectuals, for he believes that it is the performer's duty not to neglect the entertainment value of his work. "We should never lose sight of the fact that we are engaged to give *pleasure* to the audience: if at the same time we can do something to improve their taste, so much the better, but we have no right to adopt a patronizing attitude towards those who pay to hear us sing."

On the subject of contemporary music: Easton deplores the type of modern composer who writes a vocal work without bothering to study the characteristics of the voices he intends to use. This accounts for the unpopularity of several modern choral works, for choirs do not take readily to music that can be sung only with discomfort. He also thinks it is a pity that so many of our contemporary composers are afraid or incapable of writing a good tune.

Robert Easton thinks it is a pity that some choirs are reluctant to leave well alone in allowing the music they sing to speak for itself. There is the appalling notion that the works of Handel must be "improved" by the addition of stunts and tricks. The *Hallelujah* chorus, for instance, is often made quite ridiculous by stupid and conceited conductors striving after "clever" effects. As rhythm is the life-blood of all music, any effects that are desired should be obtained without altering the rhythm indicated by the composer. There is nothing clever in an "interpretation" that plays havoc with the speed of a work.

Easton is heartily in agreement with one or two other artists in this book who deplore the practice of allowing almost any sort of pianist to act as the accompanist to a guest singer. From his experience in going about the country he would say that something like 50 per cent of all the provincial recitals are spoilt by inefficient or unsuitable accompanists.

About conductors he could say a great deal more, though on the whole most of them are trying to do their jobs conscientiously. Of the greatest conductors, one of the best "accompanists" is Sir Malcolm Sargent, though Easton is also a great admirer of Sir John Barbirolli "who is unique in this country".

Of his many experiences in oratorio, one that will remain in his memory for the rest of his days is of an occasion when he took part in a performance of the *Messiah* in a large chapel in South Wales. When the soloists walked on to the platform they discovered that they were expected to sing amidst a profusion of enormous aspidistras standing in hideously-decorated pots that seemed to leer at them from their pedestals. At one stage of the proceedings, Easton had to move from the position he had taken up, and in so doing knocked one of the offending plants from its stand. It crashed on to the platform, and Easton's assurances that it had been entirely an accident were regarded with some suspicion when a few moments later the tenor was singing: "Thou shalt dash them in pieces like a potter's vessel".

"Bob" Easton, as he is known in the profession, was married in 1925 to Madeline Wadham, and has a daughter, Margaret, aged twenty-seven. They have a delightful house in Wembley Park which with its pleasant garden provides him with enough odd jobs to occupy all his spare time, though one can occasionally persuade him to play a game of billiards or table tennis.

Keith Falkner

AFTER holding some very interesting appointments, such as that of Music Officer of the British Council in Italy, this eminent singer (who for many years was regarded as one of the greatest of English vocalists), accepted a musical professorship at Cornell University and now spends the greater part of his time on the other side of the Atlantic.

He was born at Sawston, Cambridge, in 1900. At nine, he competed with sixty other boys for admission to the choir of New College, Oxford, and was one of the four chosen by Dr. (later Sir) Hugh Allen. The fine training he received in that excellent choir laid the foundation of his musical education. Practically the whole of the Bach choral music, for instance, was performed by them during his years as a chorister. The Motets, in particular, were all performed two or three times a year at Friday evensong with a choir of only eighteen boys, two altos, four tenors and four basses. In addition, a great deal of Elizabethan and modern church music was in constant use, as well as many works by such composers as Palestrina, Schütz and Handel. Most of it was performed at sight or with only one or two rehearsals.

The Great War broke into his student days, and at seventeen he joined the R.N.A.S. (the equivalent of the modern Fleet Air Arm). His period of service was uneventful apart from the excitements of early flying conditions, which were sometimes extremely hazardous. He saw only a few months of really active service: when he was engaged in submarine spotting in the English channel. It should perhaps be stated that he was awarded the Humane Society's bronze medal for life saving at sea.

On his demobilization, towards the close of 1919, he sought the advice of Sir Hugh Allen, who was at that time the Director of the Royal College of Music and who recommended him for an ex-serviceman's grant so that he could become a student of singing at the College. So for the next five years he studied there with Albert

Garcia ("a sound and fine teacher, especially for a young student") and took the organ as his second subject.

After his first year at the College, Falkner accepted an appointment as an assistant vicar-choral in the choir of St. Paul's Cathedral, which enabled him to continue his studies without economic difficulties and, at the same time, to make a start as a professional singer.

When he left St. Paul's in 1926 his voice possessed a rather lugubrious quality due, he believes, to the cavernous acoustics of that great building. A bright resonant tone, he says, was unpleasant there. To counteract this condition he became a pupil of Harry Plunket Greene, though he still continued to go to Albert Garcia from time to time. Greene's unique interpretative gifts opened up a new world for him, and it was this great teacher who made Falkner into one of the most prominent English singers of his day. "Greene's recitals still remain in my mind," Falkner declares, "they were a highlight of my musical experience."

Two other teachers made somewhat minor contributions to Falkner's success: Lierhammer, with whom he studied intermittently in Vienna and Salzburg, and Grenzebach, who gave him lessons in Berlin. Both of these teachers helped him chiefly with the classics (lieder and oratorio) and stabilized both his musical outlook and professional standing.

While he was at St. Paul's, he made various public appearances of no great importance, but in the 1925 Three Choirs Festival at Gloucester he made a very favourable impression that set him on the road to eminence. This was in Parry's *Job*, and his great success in the Lamentations he attributes largely to Plunket Greene's expert coaching.

In the same year he made his début at the promenade concerts, and from that time never lacked the sort of work he liked. The first of his many annual appearances in the Bach Choir's performances of the *St. Matthew Passion* was in 1927, and in the years that followed he was engaged at most of the English music festivals, including the Leeds Triennial.

Falkner has had many resounding successes in America, and this chapter would not be complete without mention of his appearances at the Cincinnati May Festivals in 1935, 1937 and 1939; and his annual performances with the Boston Symphony Orchestra under Koussevitzky from 1932 to 1939.

The compass of his splendidly rich and flexible voice is just over two octaves in public—E to F, but he says that in private he can manage anything between a bottom D and a top A-flat! He adds: "Not being blessed with a big voice, I have found it at times difficult to refrain from oversinging in oratorio and on other occasions when singing with an orchestra. This has sometimes caused voice strain, and I strongly advise all young singers to beware of this and never to sing 'out of their class', so to speak. Don't try to turn a clarinet into a trombone."

In the matter of breath control he mentions various points that the singing student should always bear in mind. First, it should be realized that breath control—steady emission—is the beginning and the end of the singer's technique. Secondly, the maintenance of an open throat, with the tongue low, is of the utmost importance. Thirdly, with regard to the focus of tone, there should be a gradual rising of sensation of tone as the voice rises in pitch, from top teeth to head. Finally, articulation must assist vocalization, not hinder it.

When listening to some of our younger singers he has observed many faults that good training would put right. Most of these faults come under the heading of bad production—vibrato, short phrasing and lack of tone colour; but one of the worst, he considers, is the reliance upon the natural quality of the voice in its immature state. These points can all be summed up, of course, by the statement (made by several other singers in this book) that most young singers spend too little time in study and appear before the public long before they are equipped for the job; though Mr. Falkner acknowledges that modern conditions of life are chiefly responsible for these premature efforts. To those who are thinking of taking up singing as a career he says: "DON'T, unless you are convinced that you *must*, in spite of all the difficulties". He reminds such aspirants that they must have the means, or the backing, to study hard for a minimum period of five years.

Although he would be the last to endorse all the "cranky" notions one hears about singing, he feels that we should not dismiss them all too hastily for there are some that can easily be ridiculed but which can be effective in overcoming faults if properly applied. Individual "fads" of teachers become dangerous when they are not fully understood both by the teacher and the pupil.

Falkner loves a "vibrant round voice of steady quality"—which all students should strive to acquire—but he also points out that singing means nothing to him unless it is charged with intelligence and interpretative ability. "I loathe a wobbly voice of coarse quality, and the longer I live the less I like 'emotional singing'."

His interest in folksong, the music of our great Tudors and of contemporary composers is often reflected in his song recitals, and the songs of Brahms and Schumann also occupy a prominent place in his repertoire. In oratorio, his preferences are for the works of Handel, the Bach *St. Matthew Passion* (the part of Christus) and Parry's *Job*.

Keith Falkner was married in 1930 to Miss Christabel Margaret Fullard, and they have two daughters: Julia Christabel, aged twenty-one, and Philippa Margaret, aged nineteen.

He has always been a keen sportsman, as far as his music has permitted. He has played cricket for Cambridgeshire, M.C.C. and the Free Foresters; and hockey for Middlesex and Southgate. Golf, tennis and squash must also be mentioned among his recreations; in fact, all ball games have given him great pleasure.

Sylvia Fisher

SYLVIA FISHER was almost unknown when she came to reside in England in 1947, yet within a year she had established herself as one of our leading dramatic sopranos, and was soon to have the honour of being introduced to the late Wilhelm Furtwängler by Kirsten Flagstad as "The best Sieglinde I've heard".

She was born in South Melbourne, Australia. Her father, a keen amateur singer, had emigrated from Newcastle-upon-Tyne and married an Australian girl, but unfortunately he died when his gifted daughter was very small. Sylvia's interest in music was therefore encouraged mainly by her mother, who took her to concerts and impressed upon her the necessity of studying music properly if, as she so often declared, she wished to follow in the footsteps of the many excellent singers that were to be heard in Australia in those days. Even at the age of five, Sylvia was quite sure that eventually she would become a professional singer: she would dress up in her mother's old clothes, stand before a mirror and pretend that she was taking part in the somewhat rare operatic performances that were given in her native city from time to time.

Piano lessons begun at about that time enabled her to take a prominent part in musical activities at school. She went first to a junior school in Melbourne and then to a convent school at Kilmore, some miles outside the city, where she was frequently heard in concerts given by the pupils and staff. She took the examinations of the London College of Music at that time.

On leaving school at 17 she devoted herself to the study of singing and music generally, entering the Albert Street Conservatory in Melbourne a year later. She took singing as her principal subject, with the piano, harmony and counterpoint making up the full course, which took four-and-a-half years and culminated in the winning of the full diploma with honours.

Many musical aspirants get as far as this and then discover that the greatest difficulty of all is to get even a foothold in the musical profession; indeed, the vast majority merely become local teachers of music, worthy practitioners but disappointed artists nevertheless. It is therefore interesting to note how Miss Fisher managed to get upon the somewhat precarious ladder to fame.

While still a student, she secured the part of Hermione in a performance of *Le Mariage Forcé* given at the Comedy Theatre, Melbourne, as part of the Jean Baptiste Lully tercentenary celebrations. Her outstanding performance in this rôle, in March 1932, brought her the early concert and oratorio engagements that formed the foundations of her career.

At the Conservatory her principal teacher had been Mary Campbell, a most competent musician, but Adolf Spivakovsky came to live in Melbourne at that time, and in this eminent teacher Miss Fisher found an artist equipped to give her the professional coaching she now required. She studied with him for twelve years, and during that period rose rapidly to fame in her native land, broadcasting frequently under the auspices of the Australian Broadcasting Commission. She undertook a wide range of work, including lieder recitals, but as there was no permanent opera in Melbourne, her work in this important sphere was confined mainly to broadcast productions. Her most notable successes were as Aïda, as Donna Anna in *Don Giovanni* and as Ortrud in *Lohengrin*.

By 1946 she had been heard all over Australia and was acclaimed by many as the finest soprano in the country; one newspaper referring to her as "the lineal descendant of Melba". In that year she won the "Aria competition" organised by the Melbourne newspaper *The Sun*.

Thus established in her own country, she decided to seek greater fame in England. She arrived in London in 1947, knowing very few of the prominent people in the world of music and with little idea of the many problems that beset a singer seeking to make a name in this country. She had never bothered in the least about publicity, and was a trifle disconcerted when she realised that nobody was aware of the enthusiastic reports of her performances in the Australian newspapers. To make matters worse, she found that the sudden change of climate affected her voice at first, and it was two or three months before she felt in really good form. She realised then that she had to start again from the beginning.

She asked the BBC for an audition, and as a result was engaged for a series of lieder recitals. Her great ambition to become a prima donna made her apply to Covent Garden for an audition, which in

Ibbs & Tillett

David Franklin

PLATE XIII

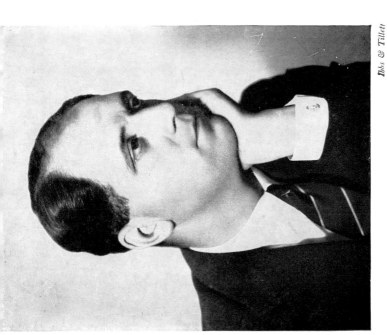

Douglas

Robert Easton

PLATE XIV

E.M.I

Kirsten Flagstad

PLATE XV

due course was granted. This led to. . . . another audition, then another, then another, and it was not until she had sung to them on five occasions that the administrators decided to engage her. Many, many criticisms have been made of the management of Covent Garden, but at least they cannot be accused of acting with undue haste in engaging Sylvia Fisher!

Her début in our national opera house was as Leonora in *Fidelio* precisely one year after her arrival in this country, which resulted in her appointment as a member of the resident company. She soon realised that singing in broadcast opera is quite a different thing from a partaking in a dramatic performance on a stage, and although her first parts were fairly small—the first Norn in *Götter-dämmerung* and the First Lady in *The Magic Flute*, for instance— many hours of patient study of the actor's art were necessary.

The year 1949 was a memorable one for her because her successes as Countess Almaviva in *The Marriage of Figaro* and as Elsa in *Lohengrin* were followed by one of her finest achievements: the Marschallin in *Der Rosenkavalier*. Her splendid interpretation of this rôle brought her into the front rank of dramatic sopranos and she then entered upon the most exacting stage in her career, for in the next few years she had to learn one rôle after another knowing full well that the public would expect the same mature impersonation in whatever part she played. The average opera-goer is generally quite unaware of the strain that a newly-arrived singer must bear when he or she has to learn a variety of principal parts in quick succession: every rôle has its own unique problems to be overcome quite apart from the feat of memorisation, and Miss Fisher soon found herself working and studying anything up to eighteen hours a day. On top of all this she had to cope with all the irritating little difficulties of everyday life, for she still had few friends in London who could be called upon for help. How she longed for a few hours respite to give some thought to the choice of dressmaker and hair-dresser, and to the furnishing of her flat! She still recalls quite vividly how she almost fainted at a rehearsal and then suddenly realised that she had not eaten a proper meal for three days. Know-ing this, her achievements during this trying period seem all the more remarkable: Elsa in *Lohengrin*, Gutrune, Brünnhilde and Sieglinde in *Die Walküre*, Isolde in *Tristan und Isolde*, Elisabeth in *Tannhäuser*, Agathe in *Der Freischütz*, Senta in *Der Fliegende Holländer*, Kostelnicka in *Jenufa* and Ursula in *Mathis der Maler*,—all had to be mastered quickly, for her successes at Covent Garden inevitably brought demands from opera houses abroad and for a variety of concert performances.

In March 1952 she made her début as a guest artiste at the Teatro dell' Opera in Rome during the International Season, under the conductorship of Dr. Erich Kleiber, giving a most satisfying performance of Sieglinde. Other notable successes abroad include her Isolde in Sicily and Gutrune in Bologna.

The following year brought another ordeal: the singing of Isolde at Covent Garden in succession to Kirsten Flagstad. Fortunately she was able to go to Berlin for a while to study it under that distinguished Isolde of the nineteen-thirties, Frida Leider, and she returned to give an exquisite and moving interpretation, worthy of her illustrious predecessor.

During these years she was also distinguishing herself as a concert artiste, her first Promenade Concert coming soon after her début at Covent Garden. It would be impossible to give details of all these performances, but mention should be made of her beautiful singing of the principal soprano parts of such works as the Bach B-minor Mass, the Beethoven Ninth Symphony, the great Requiems of Verdi and Brahms, and the Mass of Life (Delius), of which a memorable performance was given under the direction of Sir Thomas Beecham. Her repertoire of German lieder includes more than three hundred items, the majority having been prepared for broadcast recitals, but she is also interested in a wide range of songs, including French, Italian, American and Spanish as well as English and Australian.

In December 1954 she had the honour of creating the rôle of Cressida in the world première of Sir William Walton's opera *Troilus and Cressida*, and while modern works are being considered it should be mentioned that she was a most convincing Ellen Orford in Benjamin Britten's *Peter Grimes*, at Covent Garden and later at Wiesbaden.

During the spring and early summer of 1955 she returned to her native country for the first time in seven years to give a prolonged tour of the principal centres of musical activity, discovering that her achievements at Covent Garden had greatly enhanced her reputation at home. One critic declared that the rapturous beauty of her singing equalled that of Lotte Lehmann; the *Sun* noted that even after years of strain in operatic work she could still sing with the freshness of a young girl; the *Argus* referred to her "almost faultless technique".

Back in Britain again she continued to win the approval of the critics, whose comments upon her most recent efforts are note-worthy. The critic of the *Daily Telegraph* wrote on October 31st 1955: "A good performance of the opera (*Der Rosenkavalier*) should be dominated by the Marschallin. Sylvia Fisher, expert in the part, was both dignified and touching—her Act I curtain brought tears to the eyes." The critic of *The Times* declared that she could not easily be bettered in the part of Elisabeth in *Tannhäuser*, and when this opera was repeated in April 1956 the *Daily Telegraph* commented: "Elizabeth is an advantageous rôle for that great singer Sylvia Fisher's principal attribute, the sweetness of her voice. In the Prayer she held the large audience spellbound".

One of her more recent successes was in *Turandot* in May 1957. Writing in the *Daily Telegraph*, Martin Cooper declared: "The title rôle in Puccini's *Turandot* makes almost unique demands on the high dramatic soprano voice and to undertake it is an act of bravery in itself. Sylvia Fisher carried it off at Covent Garden on Saturday with extraordinary aplomb. The part certainly lies within her voice and she showed herself mistress of its broad sweeping phrases . . . . Her words were admirably clear and if she can propel them with more convincing violence of intention her Turandot will be a great achievement."

Later in the same year she triumphed again as Brünnhilde in *Die Walküre*, thus gaining the distinction of being the first British artist to sing this arduous rôle at Covent Garden since the war.

It is perhaps the beauty and purity of her tone, together with the fact that she can achieve a really dramatic *fortissimo* climax without forcing her voice, that has accounted for her success in the realm of opera. Of the utmost importance, too, is her ability to sing for hours with perfect intonation, an accomplishment too rarely found among Wagnerian sopranos. She has a compass of well over three octaves, with wonderful warmth and colour even towards the extremities. Moreover, her control of it is so firm that she can produce a seemingly-endless variety of beautifully shaded tones.

She has no fanciful notions about singing but, on the other hand, does not agree with those who seem to think that anyone can teach her art. There are plenty of competent teachers who can put a promising singer on the road to success, but the one thing that must be avoided at all costs is the danger of placing too great a strain upon a youthful voice. The temptation to do too much is one that every young singer must constantly resist because once the bloom has gone off a voice it can never be regained. Very few voices can stand up to the strain of operatic work for long unless this restraint is practised, in fact maturity is essential for Wagnerian and other heavy rôles. Many a promising young voice has been ruined in an opera house because its owner would not refuse a part that was too heavy or strenuous: a singer must know the limitations of his or her own voice.

Sylvia Fisher was married in 1953 to an Italian violinist, Ubaldo Gardini of Bologna. They met in Florence during one of her tours abroad. Soon after their marriage, Miss Fisher fulfilled a long-standing ambition: the acquisition of a "house of character". With her husband's help she found a delightful property in Bayswater and then embarked upon the exciting adventure of furnishing it mainly with antiques. It was then that they discovered what it costs to live in a reasonable manner in these inflationary times. However, her husband found an Italian cook with a gift for making life worth living, and they were soon entertaining their friends with such Italian hospitality that their house became known as the Little-Bologna-in-Bayswater. Miss Fisher often looks back on her bachelor-flat-and-sandwich days and sighs with contentment.

Although much of her leisure is still being spent in buying pictures and additional furnishings for "Little Bologna", she likes to get out into the country whenever it is possible to indulge her love for all forms of nature, for at heart she is still an Australian with a deep feeling for wild country. She recalls that only a few years ago she drove several thousands of miles through the bush to appreciate the grandeur of her native land. Her many Australian friends need never fear that she will forget them.

Kirsten Flagstad

WE seldom hear Kirsten Flagstad in person today, but through the medium of the gramophone we are able to refresh our memories of one of the few really great Wagnerian sopranos of the twentieth century. She possesses a "heaven-sent" voice that carried her rapidly to fame as soon as she was heard outside her native country. It is such a majestic and luxurious voice that she could, if she wished, captivate her audiences with little display of artistry; but her fame in the opera house rests upon a combination of qualities. Hers is not only a magnificent voice: it has remarkable staying power and is produced, it seems, with extraordinary ease. Her vocal technique is excellent and her powers of interpretation leave little to be desired. Now in this country we have one or two voices comparable with Flagstad's in quality or volume, but they cannot stand up to a whole evening of Wagner. We have voices with remarkable powers of endurance, but they lack the quality. There are one or two singers whose technique, quite frankly, is rather better than Flagstad's but these talented singers of ours lack the magnificent voice! Flagstad is therefore richly endowed on all points, and until we can produce a super-soprano of the dramatic type in this country, we must acknowledge that she is unmatched in these islands.

She was born at Hamar, near Oslo, on 2 July 1895 into an intensely musical environment: her father was a conductor in the operetta and orchestral sphere and her mother was a good pianist. She began to learn to play the piano at a very early age and seemed to be singing all day long, for whenever she attended a light opera conducted by her father she returned home quite enthralled, with the songs ringing in her mind. Visits to occasional productions of grand opera were even more exciting, and most of her leisure hours as a girl were spent in learning arias to be sung purely for her own enjoyment.

Her parents were anxious that she should be trained for a medical career—it did not seem to occur to them that she might rise to fame as a singer, despite the fact that even in girlhood she possessed an extremely beautiful voice—what is commonly called "a natural voice".

However, Kirsten began to sing in light operas and it soon became evident to everybody that she had a future as an opera singer. She was only eighteen when she made her professional début at the National Theatre, Oslo, as Nuri in *Tiefland*, an opera by d'Albert that is almost unknown today. Her success was such that a number of her friends formed a little committee to provide her parents with financial aid for her musical education.

Three teachers were in turn responsible for her training: Ellen Schytte-Jacobsen (with whom she studied for three years in Oslo), Albert Westwang, and Dr. Gillis-Bratt of Stockholm. Her progress during the next few years was not spectacular: she continued to sing in light opera and to make a modest reputation as an oratorio singer, but in those days there seemed to be little prospect of making an international reputation.

She married in 1919 and had a daughter a year later. Music-lovers in Oslo feared that domestic responsibilities would mean the end of her promising career, but in 1921 she returned to public life and made a particularly successful concert tour in Norway. On returning to Oslo she accepted a contract with the Mayol Theatre there, and for the next two years played a prominent part in their comic opera productions.

Concert engagements from time to time also continued to enhance her reputation, but for the next ten years or so she still remained unknown outside her native country. In 1928 she joined the company at the Stora Theatre, Gothenburg, and then began to concentrate upon grand opera.

Good progress was being made when in 1930 her friends again had reason to fear that she might withdraw from public life, for she married for the second time, her previous union having been dissolved. She now became the wife of Henry Johansen, a wealthy citizen of Oslo, and for the next two years was rarely heard in public.

In 1932, however, she made a tremendous "hit" as Isolde: a success that aroused interest in several operatic circles in Germany, and as a result she was invited to Bayreuth in the following year to join the company at the famous festival theatre built by Wagner himself. Her first season there was spent in playing minor rôles to get accustomed to the peculiar "atmosphere" of the theatre, its traditions and outlook, but in 1934 she was given the chance of playing Sieglinde in *Die Walküre*, and once again made a very favourable impression.

Reports of her performance reached America, and early in the following year she made her début at the Metropolitan Opera House, New York. As Sieglinde she won the hearts of everybody, but the sensation of the season came a few days later when her impersonation of Isolde sent the critics into raptures. She had been engaged for only one season, but the administrators of the Opera House hastened to prepare a contract that would keep this new star of opera on their side of the Atlantic for at least a season in each of the years to come.

So when Flagstad came to Covent Garden in 1936 she was recognized as one of the world's greatest opera singers, and the audiences at the Royal Opera House expected from her a very high standard of performance. They could scarcely have been disappointed. Her Isolde was not to be compared with anything that had been heard in recent years, and as Brünnhilde she was beyond criticism.

In June of the same year she gave a magnificent recital at the Queen's Hall, and some idea of her performance when shorn of the splendour of the opera house may be gained from the July issue of the *Musical Times*. Writing of the recital, Mr. William McNaught declared: "Her voice is of exceptional power, beauty and suppleness, her style ranges from majesty to quiet serenity, even coyness, and her technique can encompass any feat of movement and poise, whether energetic or tranquil. . . . Madame Flagstad's singing was that of a highly-gifted, well-practised and intelligent artist, who adds to her artistic qualities that of personal magnetism. Forty years ago, perhaps, it would not have stood alone; but in the present state of singing it is what we call epoch-making."

Her début in Vienna was made at about the same time, and in 1937 she was back at Covent Garden again. A tour of Australia was made in 1938 and in May of the following year she was fulfilling important engagements at the New York World's Fair.

In more recent years she has made many welcome re-appearances at Covent Garden. Those who were privileged to be present will for a long time remember the splendid performance of *Tristan and*

Isolde early in 1948 when with a worthy supporting cast she sang before the most distinguished audience the Royal Opera House had attracted for years. The Queen was present, with Princess Elizabeth, the Duke of Edinburgh, Princess Margaret and the Duchess of Kent. There were twenty curtain calls, the last of which Madame Flagstad took amidst a blaze of bouquets.

The glory of her voice—that smooth, steady flow of really lovely tone—was never more evident than in the broadcast of *Alceste* in the Third Programme in April 1956, and many a listener must have wished that she could be persuaded to give us a few more reminders of her consummate artistry.

Another recent performance of hers that lingers in the memory was when she sang a number of songs by Grieg at the Grieg Anniversary Promenade Concert at the Albert Hall in September 1957.

Kirsten Flagstad's voice possesses an enormous compass and it seems to be quite full even at its extremities. Its upper part, particularly, is wonderfully rich and resonant, and she has no difficulty in singing across even an "open" orchestra of full Wagnerian dimensions.

In her time she has played over seventy rôles, including the many comic opera parts she sang in her native land, but it is as a Wagnerian singer that she will take her place in the history of song. Her greatest rôles have been Isolde, Brünnhilde, Sieglinde, Elsa, Elizabeth, Kundry and Senta, but she has also impersonated Aïda, Eurydice and Marguerite very impressively.

A word must also be added about Madame Flagstad's work outside the opera house, because she has proved herself to be one of the most charming recitalists ever heard in London. In lieder she makes us realize what it is to be "born a singer" and one could scarcely wish for anything more delightful than her rendering of Scandinavian songs.

In private life, Madame Flagstad is a retiring personality and can rarely be enticed to take part in social events. Many of our prominent opera singers revel in parties and, despite fatigue, will indulge in merry-making "after the show" until the grey of dawn reminds them that only a few hours hence they will be singing again. Kirsten Flagstad strongly disapproves of such practices, believing that a singer must have adequate rest in sleep and, in addition, recreation of mind and body in order to endure the strain of being "keyed up" to concert pitch night after night.

Similarly, she believes that an excess of luxury is bound to have a detrimental effect upon any artist, and therefore she leads a quiet and modest, if not austere, life doing many of her "odd jobs" herself. She is not "temperamental" and never adopts a supercilious attitude towards minor members of the cast; indeed, many a time has she given valuable advice to even the most humble members of the company.

David Franklin

THERE are times when every schoolmaster surveys the professions of his friends and dreams wistfully of freedom from grubby little boys and smudgy exercise books. Those who quit teaching generally take the easy course of acquiring a dog-collar, which, if they are of suitable age, may possibly provide a short cut to an episcopal apron, much to the annoyance of sundry canons and embittered archdeacons who, having worked their way up from humble curacies, feel that they are better qualified to become lords spiritual than any wordly pedagogue.

David Franklin did not take the easy way out, and for that matter, he wasn't even looking for an escape from Smith minor: he became an opera singer almost by chance, though one feels that sooner or later his fine bass voice would have inevitably taken him far from the Junior Common Room.

He is a Londoner, born in 1908 and educated at Alleyn's School, Dulwich. A choral scholarship took him to St. Catharine's College, Cambridge, in 1927, where for three years he read English and History, and in due course took an honours degree. As an undergraduate he took part in many of the University's musical activities, though he claims that one of the most significant things he did at Cambridge was to cause the cancellation of a certain "musical activity". At St. Catharine's it was customary to sing the Merbecke setting of the Communion service at seven o'clock every morning—a misery to the singers if not to the other members of the college—and Franklin complained that it was unreasonable to expect young baritone and bass voices to sing such a high *tessitura* at such an hour. It was therefore decided that in future the service would be said.

In 1930 David Franklin became a master at Sutton Valence School, and for five years pumped English, History and Latin into Smith minor. During these years he was a "happy amateur" as far as music was concerned: he sang in the school choir and organized various concerts for the edification of scholars and staff alike,

Then there were frequent dramatic performances which he produced very successfully, and the O.T.C., of which he was the Com-
mander. One gathers that the rest of his time was his own.

During his holidays he became very interested in a small organization that was running "musical camps" for young professional and
amateur musicians who were sufficiently enthusiastic to spend a
few weeks under canvas in the summer so that they could indulge in
mutual music-making. It was at one of these camps that he became
acquainted with Miss Ursula Nettleship, the Chelsea singing
teacher. One day, she said to him: "You are going to be invited to
sing in a Nativity Play at a church in Chelsea. I should be glad if
you would accept the engagement". This sort of thing did not really
interest him, but he accepted, and it led, a few months' later, to his
being offered an engagement to sing the four small bass parts in a
performance of the Bach *St. Matthew Passion* at Lewes. He says he
sang them "louder and rougher than they had ever been sung
before", but that is beside the point. What really matters is that
when fulfilling this engagement he stayed for a few nights with Mr.
and Mrs. John Christie at Glyndebourne and that after dinner one
evening he sang an aria from *The Magic Flute*. Little comment was
made at the time, but eight or nine months later he was offered an
audition with Fritz Busch in London, and as a result, was given an
engagement to sing the part of the Commendatore in *Don Giovanni*
at Glyndebourne in the following summer—1936. Within four
days of this audition he was in Vienna studying with Jani Strasser,
an excellent teacher with whom he worked for the next four years.

It now became necessary to resign his scholastic appointment,
and once again it was Miss Ursula Nettleship who helped him, for
she organized a maintenance fund to tide him over the transitional
period. His first season at Glyndebourne was an encouraging
success, and he played there each subsequent year until the outbreak of war. His chief rôles, apart from the Commendatore, were
Sarastro in *The Magic Flute* and Banco in Verdi's *Macbeth*. During
those years he was, in addition, building up a considerable reputation as a concert singer, doing the usual sort of oratorio work and
broadcasting. In 1939 he also took part in the Mozart Festivals at
Antwerp and Brussels, where he appeared not only as the Commendatore, but as Dr. Bartolo in *Figaro*.

Then came the war, and as Franklin had always held a Territorial
commission, his musical career was brought to an abrupt end. He

served in turn on the staffs of the Scottish, Northern Ireland and South-Eastern commands, and during the intensive activity in the planning of the Second Front his health broke down and he was taken to hospital. When he was discharged in 1944 he held the rank of Major.

He was still very ill when he returned to civilian life and it would have been impossible to resume such a strenuous career as that of a professional singer immediately: the continual travelling, for one thing, would have probably put him back into hospital again. So for eighteen months he worked as secretary to the headmaster of St. Albans School, and came up to London three evenings a week for lessons with Strasser.

Then he undertook a series of Arts Council concerts, various broadcasts, and a fair amount of provincial oratorio work, thus gradually getting back into his stride. A welcome opportunity to return to the opera stage came when he was invited to sing as a guest artist with the Sadler's Wells Company during their nine-week tour in Germany for the benefit of the troops. Incidentally, while he was in Berlin he found an old magazine bearing Adolf Hitler's bookplate near the air-raid shelter in the Chancellery grounds. This little memento is now framed above the fireplace in the study of his London house.

In the summer of 1946 Franklin signed a contract as a principal bass with the Covent Garden Opera Company, and in November of that year commenced his duties there. The first part he was given took precisely forty-five seconds to sing! This was of course to give him time to learn a more important rôle: Baron Ochs in *Der Rosenkavalier*. It had been known for basses to take anything up to a year to memorize Ochs, and some people think that Franklin set up a new record by memorizing one hundred and eighty pages of this most difficult music in less than three months.

As Baron Ochs, Sarastro in *The Magic Flute*, Sparafucile in *Rigoletto*, Pogner in the *Mastersingers* and Hunding in *The Valkyrie*, he became well-known in the world of opera. Believing that an opera singer should have a certain amount of work to do outside the theatre to keep him "balanced" musically he accepted many broadcasting engagements as well as occasional oratorio work. He has sung in such works as the *Messiah*, *Judas Maccabaeus*, *Samson*, *Saul*, *The Dream of Gerontius*, the *Creation*, the two Bach *Passions* and the B minor Mass, and has been heard in many of the Third Programme broadcasts of the music of Purcell, and in lieder. He may be heard in the HMV recording of *Don Giovanni* (ALP 1199-1201).

To students of singing, Franklin would say that diction is half the battle, for it is impossible to seize the attention of an audience if they cannot hear your words. One cannot do better than follow the example of a fine artist like Percy Hemming, whose diction was famous and immaculate.

He considers that one of the most important things a professional singer should know is when to say "no". It is asking for trouble to take on too much work. Every musician should also realize that the day will never come when he need no longer study. "When the artist has no more to learn he's ready to die." Carl Ebert said that to Franklin at Glyndebourne in 1939 and he has never forgotten it.

David Franklin's voice ranges from C to F-sharp—nearly two-and-a-half octaves. Eric Blom has described it as "a great and noble voice", and it is certainly in keeping with his person, for he is tall and powerfully built. To these assets he adds a fine sense of drama and faultless musicianship, and thus his success in the opera house is accounted for.

He was married in 1931 to Mary Bickell, and has two daughters who share his love of music. At home, the music room is the centre of all activity, in fact he finds the greatest difficulty in getting it to himself when there is rehearsing to be done. His recreations are the theatre, politics and books; his reading being chiefly of biography, good modern fiction—satirical for preference—and anything else of outstanding merit.

Eric Greene

ERIC Greene is the third prominent figure of that surname in English musical history, but although he spells his name with a final "e", as did Maurice Greene and Harry Plunket Greene, he is no relation to either of them. A high lyric tenor, he has won his laurels almost exclusively in oratorio and song, and today he is one of the best Bach tenors we possess.

He is a Londoner, born in 1903. His mother was fairly well known as a contralto under her professional name, Isobel Wallace Wilson, and frequently played the handbells in variety shows as Isobel Wallace, "The Campanologist". At one time, his father was a tenor in the choir of the Chapel Royal, Sandringham, but became better known to the general public when during the Great War he toured the halls in a musical act called "The Four Tommies".

Eric Greene was one of nine children: seven boys and two girls; all musical. And for the benefit of superstitious people it can be said that he was the seventh son of a seventh son! As a boy, most of his spare time was spent either in playing the piano or mooning about pensively; hence his nickname "The Dreamer". Perhaps the most vivid memory of his early days is of the annual concert that his family used to give in North London in aid of charity. All eleven members took part, and in one year they made as much as £1,900. He also has recollections of himself as a smart little fellow in an Eton suit accompanying his sister Dorothy (who won a singing scholarship to the Royal Academy of Music) when she sang at some of the National Sunday League concerts.

At ten, Eric Greene won a choral scholarship to Winchester Cathedral, where he was a solo boy for the greater part of his five-and-a-half years as a chorister. Most musical boys who find themselves in a cathedral are attracted towards the organ, and Greene was no exception. When Dr. Prendergast, the Cathedral organist, discovered that this bright lad could play tolerably well, he took an interest in him and eventually accepted him as an organ pupil. Thus towards the end of his time at Winchester he was allowed to

ERIC GREENE

take choir practices and even play the cathedral organ for some of the less important services. He recalls playing at some of the Sunday evening services for members of the armed forces.

His ambition in those days was divided between becoming a cathedral organist and an orchestral conductor, but when he left school the prospect of earning a living in music was not particularly bright, so at seventeen he joined the staff of the Westminster Bank at the head office in Lothbury E.C.2, where in time he became secretary to the Chief Controller, and contemporary of John Wilmot, a former Minister of Supply.

At about the same time as his entry into the banking profession, Greene became organist of St. Peter's, Great Windmill Street, a useful appointment that enabled him to continue his musical studies in his leisure hours. He also joined a male voice quartet in which Maurice Evans, who later went to America, was the alto. Of their many adventures, one of the most interesting was when they dressed as artisans and sang to a theatre queue to raise money for charity. This was not quite such a simple matter as it sounds, for it necessitated getting permission from the "regulars" who occupied all the best pitches, otherwise there would have been trouble! In a single evening they made twenty-eight pounds, which suggests that the music-hall jokes about there being as much money outside the theatre as inside are not as far-fetched as one would suppose.

Another important step forward was made when Eric Greene got a scholarship to the Royal Academy of Music. No sooner had he heard of the award than in an interview with Sir Alexander Mackenzie, the principal at that time, he learnt that as he was working in a bank he could not be admitted to the Academy. Seeing the young man's disappointment, Mackenzie proceeded to compromise by saying that if he could do anything else besides sing he would try to make an exception in his case. Greene immediately played first the organ and then the piano to him, and Mackenzie made special arrangements for him so that he could commence his studies each afternoon at four o'clock. (Greene believes that his is the only case in which such arrangements have ever been made). At the Westminster Bank they generously gave him time off so that he could fall in with this plan, and for the next three-and-a-half years he was a business man until tea-time and a music student afterwards.

95

His first opportunity to shine as a singer came in 1927 when Sir Henry Wood chose him for the Evangelist's part in a performance of the Bach *St. Matthew Passion* to be given at the Queen's Hall by the students of the Academy. His execution of this difficult part made Sir Henry realize that he was a good Bach tenor in the making, and from that time he gave Greene personal tuition, chiefly in the sphere of musical appreciation and interpretation. He also took him about the country to illustrate his lectures on singing, and Greene was frequently called upon to demonstrate the difference between good and "throaty" production. It was Wood, by the way, who gave him his first important professional engagement: to sing in *The Apostles* at a performance given by the Leicester Philharmonic Society.

At the Westminster Bank he re-formed their Operatic and Orchestral Societies, building them up to five hundred strong and conducting their productions at the Scala Theatre.

In 1936 he received a most exciting offer: to make a six months' tour of Central Europe with the New English Singers under the direction of Cuthbert Kelly. The Westminster Bank once again rose to the occasion by giving him leave of absence to accept the invitation.

Plenty could be written about this tour, but mention can be made here of but one interesting experience they had. In Germany they hoped to have an opportunity of singing to Hitler; our ambassador having made the necessary approach. For five days they were kept in Berlin while arrangements were being made, and finally they heard that 11-30 a.m. on 1 May had been fixed. It was therefore a great surprise when they heard at the last minute that Hitler could not hear them because he had to go to Munich for the May Day celebrations. It seemed very strange, and then it began to dawn upon them that their bodyguard of a couple of Stormtroopers, who followed them wherever they went, had not been provided out of any anxiety for their safety, but to see if they were engaged in what might be regarded as "fifth column" activity. When they left Germany they found it difficult to suppress a suspicion that the negotiations were prolonged deliberately as an excuse for their detention in Berlin, and that it had never been Hitler's intention to hear them.

On his return to England, Greene found the demand for his services growing every day, and it became necessary to make a

ERIC GREENE

choice between a career in banking and in music. He decided on the latter with somewhat mixed feelings, for he was deeply conscious of the consideration shown to him by the Westminster Bank, and this goes to prove that our banks are not the soulless, mercenary institutions that some writers would have us believe! One gets rather tired of irresponsible novelists who portray banks as dens of ruthless capitalist iniquity staffed by servile individuals whose personalities have been destroyed by monotonous clerical work and toadying to the rich. Actually, the banking profession attracts an unusually high percentage of well-read, intelligent men and women who know how to combine scrupulous honesty with good manners, which is more than one can say about the profession of politics.

However, to return to Mr. Eric Greene: he had the honour of singing in the choir at the coronation of King George VI and Queen Elizabeth, and found himself next to Ben Davis and John Coates. The singers who on this great occasion augmented the regular choir of Westminster Abbey were chosen personally by the late Sir Walford Davies, who was then Master of the King's Music.

Greene then toured America and Canada with the New English Singers. and while he was in the United States he secured several odd engagements that gave him some idea of the earning power of a good voice in the wealthiest country in the world. For a single ten-minute broadcast he received a staggering fee from Messrs. Heinz, the gentlemen who provide us with baked beans and certain other commodities. For some time afterwards, Greene's friends called him the Fifty-eighth Variety.

When one considers the colossal fees that can be squeezed out of the sponsors of America's commercial radio network by the more exacting type of artist (Greene, it appears, did not haggle: it seemed too good to be true)—one begins to realize what a tremendous temptation lies across the Atlantic for those who are fairly confident of success. We should bear this in mind when we complain about the comparatively modest fees demanded by the greater British artists who are content to spend their time in this land of many hardships. It should be remembered of course that these fantastically-paid artists have to possess ready-made "names", unless they are of the hard-boiled jazz variety, in which case an ability to make suggestive noises in the course of a boisterously rendered song can compensate for the lack of everything else.

97

During the Second World War, Eric Greene and his wife—whom we shall meet later—were among the first artists to sing at a factory concert. When C.E.M.A. came into being he was appointed as their organizer in the counties of Devon and Cornwall, where for six months he arranged and took part in concerts in village halls, factories, hostels, etc. Then he became the Regional Officer for the East and West Ridings of Yorkshire and continued the good work in the north. He took part in over six hundred factory concerts while he held this appointment.

In August 1944 he was sent to the Orkneys to visit the Home Fleet (including the battleships *King George V* and the *Duke of York*) and units of the Russian fleet at Scapa Flow. Under the fifteen-inch guns of the *Archangel* he sang unaccompanied Elizabethan music to a large assembly of men of the Russian Navy and was told by Admiral Ivanov that the music was so beautiful that they hoped to hear a lot more before long. They gave him vodka for tea, by the way, which few singers would choose as an afternoon drink!

One of his last activities with C.E.M.A., which he left in 1944, was when he sang with the Jacques String Orchestra at the reopening of the famous old Theatre Royal, Bristol. With Dr. Jacques, he was afterwards presented to the Queen.

Eric Greene, who is now a Fellow of the Royal Academy of Music, has a pleasantly serene voice with a compass of about two-and-a-half octaves, reaching up to top C, and is probably heard at his best in the oratorios of Bach. He has performed the *St. Matthew Passion* over five hundred times, and on one never-to-be-forgotten occasion played the continuo at the same time! In recital work he is specializing in English song, and it is all to his credit that he gives so much attention to works of our glorious Tudor period.

He is strongly of the opinion that all singers should be able to play the piano tolerably well, otherwise they are severely handicapped in studying complicated work.

A singer should also concern himself with the development of his own country's characteristics in music, he declares, and it need scarcely be added that he is a great believer in English music; in fact, he is deeply appreciative of all forms of English art.

He denies that choral singing is declining in this country, but admits that it is changing in a variety of ways, and that more young

ERIC GREENE

people must be attracted to the choral societies if the latter are to continue their great traditions. The efforts of Dr. Jacques to interest school children in this form of musical activity are particularly commendable.

Membership of a choral society, he points out, is one of the best forms of training for those who aspire to solo work, and it can also be very helpful to those who are experiencing difficulty in sight-reading. The chief thing to remember is to resist the temptation to shout and to overwork the voice.

For male singers, a training as a cathedral chorister is a foundation of inestimable value. To be able to sing the psalms beautifully, as they try to do in most cathedrals, is to have mastered most of the principles of good singing. Alas! no boy can confidently predict what his voice will be like in manhood, and that is perhaps why the value of a cathedral training is not always appreciated at the time by those who enjoy it.

Eric Greene was married in 1942 to Mary Linde, the soprano, who for some years was a member of the Sadler's Wells Company under the name of Dorothy Kingston. They frequently sing duets together.

A love of other arts, besides music, forms one of Greene's outstanding characteristics, for he is a good judge of paintings, having some of Reginald Haggar's water colours and some pleasing specimens of Marjorie Incledon's work in oils; he likes pottery and collects antique furniture, chiefly of the Regency period. He has a tidy, analytical mind, and reads mostly autobiographies, historical works and books on music. Perhaps one should also add that he is a heavy pipe-smoker (he finds it harmless to his voice, but points out that this might not be the case with other people!) and, curiously enough, is fond of housework. Most women would call him an ideal husband! His wife testifies to the fact that he is an excellent cook and can also be very handy when there are redecorations to be done.

In his earlier days he played a fair amount of football, but in more recent times, swimming has been his chief outdoor recreation, with the exception of walking on the Sussex downs with his wife. Whenever they get an entirely free day they set out at eight in the morning and tramp for miles.

Hilde Güden

THE amazing development of the recording industry in recent years, chiefly as a result of the invention of the long-playing record, has vastly increased the number of music-lovers in this country who are quite familiar with the names and voices of eminent singers whose personal appearances here are rare. That fascinating and beautiful dramatic soprano Hilde Güden, therefore, needs little introduction.

She was born in Vienna just before the end of the Great War. Her father was devoted to music, but it was probably from her mother Frida Brammer, once a student at the Vienna State Academy of Drama, that she inherited her love of opera, for everything theatrical was a source of delight to her even as a very small child.

In those days, the majority of middle-class Viennese children learned to play the piano, and her parents certainly did not realise that they were laying the foundations of a distinguished career in music when they encouraged her to start lessons at the age of seven. Although she was evidently a talented child, it was not until after she had started to study singing in earnest at the age of fourteen that some indication of her abilities became apparent. At sixteen she gave an astonishingly accomplished performance in a light operetta, but even after this she was still doubtful about taking up music professionally. This diffidence was not shared by her mother, however, who soon convinced her that her success in operetta justified serious study of singing and dramatic art, including dancing. So she went to the Max Reinhardt school, and also became a pupil at the Vienna Conservatory, her principal teacher being Madame Wetzelsberger. Just before the outbreak of war in 1939 she had a foretaste of the triumphs she was later to enjoy when she took part in a Viennese production of *Hearts in the Snow*.

Her mother was of Jewish origin, and in order to escape from the Nazi oppression, the family moved to Switzerland. So beautiful and gifted a girl could scarcely remain unnoticed for long, and it is not surprising that she attracted the attention of Robert Denzler, the director of the Zürich Opera House. He was planning a new production of *Figaro* and was looking for a Cherubino possessing not only an adequate voice and the requisite musical ability but youthful freshness, an attractive boyish face and a real feeling for the part of the roguish page-boy. In Hilde Güden he found everything. It was a sensational début: she melted the hearts of even the sternest critics, and the audiences were captivated. Here, they all agreed, was a Cherubino that Mozart would have loved. She became a member of the company, and stayed in Zürich two years singing many of the principal rôles in the repertoire.

In 1941 she was invited to sing at the Munich State Opera, and having been given the assurances she required, she made her first appearance in this famous opera house as Zerlina in *Don Giovanni*, under the direction of Clemens Krauss. Here again, the casting was perfect: one could have scoured the whole world for a singer without finding one more fitted for the part of the pretty, coquettish peasant girl. Richard Strauss was in the audience, and to Hilde Güden's surprise he came to her dressing-room after the performance and said he would like her to play the part of Sophie in his famous opera *Der Rosenkavalier*. She immediately agreed to study it, little knowing that this was to become her most successful rôle. He never missed an opportunity to admire her in this part, and always addressed her afterwards as "My Sophie".

It was as Sophie that she made her début at the Teatro Reale in Rome in December 1942; another great impersonation that would have led to world-wide fame almost at once but for the war, which by this time was making it extremely difficult to move from country to country.

The year 1946 brought her first opportunity to shine at the famous Salzburg Festival, which set the seal of greatness upon her career. Since that year she has been recognised as a soprano of international repute. She became a member of the Vienna State Opera in 1947 and in the following year made her first appearance at La Scala, Milan.

Her début at Covent Garden was with the Vienna State Opera company in 1947 as Zerlina. When she appeared as Cherubino shortly afterwards the London audience was enchanted: here was a really boyish character with an impish sense of humour and a really thrilling voice, clear, smooth and firm. They noticed the exceptional quality of her upper register, her graceful phrasing and the superb ease with which she poured forth her colourful notes. For her American début at the Metropolitan Opera House in 1951 she agreed to appear as Gilda in *Rigoletto*: a little surprising, because this has never been one of her best parts. Nevertheless, she enjoyed a resounding success and since then has enjoyed many ovations in that celebrated theatre. Incidentally, she played this part at Covent Garden during her visit to this country in 1956. Another of her outstanding performances at the Metropolitan was her Eurydice in Gluck's *Orfeo and Eurydice* in 1955: it was one of the most sympathetic interpretations of this part within living memory.

There is insufficient space in this short biography for a catalogue of her many achievements at Salzburg, but a mention, at least, should be made of her vivid personification of Norina in *Don Pasquale* (Donizetti). This opera is not a great work of art musically, but it affords delightful opportunities for a soprano with a real sense of comedy, and Hilde Güden certainly made the most of them. It will be recalled that Norina, a most attractive young widow, goes through a mock marriage with old Don Pasquale, posing first as a docile girl brought up in a convent. The old rascal is quickly disillusioned, for soon after the "ceremony" is over, Norina becomes a very naughty girl and eventually drives him almost crazy with her unruly ways and incredible extravagance. Hilde Güden played the part with a mischievous zest that was quite irresistible.

Her interest in modern opera is noteworthy. She has appeared in *The Rape of Lucretia* (Benjamin Britten) Hindemith's *Mathis der Maler* and *The Rake's Progress* (Stravinsky), for instance, and being a keen student of music (which is more than can be said for most of the great sopranos of yesterday) is always willing to consider an exacting part in a work from a contemporary pen if she considers that it is worthy of the name of opera. She has no fear of technical difficulties, and can stand the strain of high coloratura rôles. Although she has always been able to speak several languages, she did not seem entirely happy in singing in English until a few years ago. She prefers singing in German, French or Italian.

Her recordings are so numerous that it is impossible to give details of them all in the space available here, but she can be heard in many complete operas such as Donizetti's *L'Elisir* (LXT 5155-7), *Figaro* (LXT 5088-91), *Don Giovanni* (LXT 5103-6), *The Magic Flute* (LXT 5085-7), *La Bohème* (LXT 2622-3), *Fledermaus* (LXT

HILDE GÜDEN

2550-1), *Rosenkavalier* (LXT 2954-7), *The Rake's Progress* (ABI 3055-7), *Rigoletto* (LXT 5006-8), and *Meistersinger* (LXT 2659-64). She can also be heard in a recording of Beethoven's Ninth Symphony (LXT 2725-6) with the Vienna Philharmonic Orchestra conducted by Kleiber.

Joan Hammond

MISS Joan Hammond is one of those people who are born to achieve distinction in some way. If she had not chosen to become a singer, this dynamic personality could easily have won fame as a sportswoman or, but for an unfortunate accident that injured her left hand, as a violinist. For some years she was also a successful journalist.

She is an Australian, though her birth actually took place at Christchurch, New Zealand in 1912. Her home was at Sydney, New South Wales, where her father was in business and where she received her education. At school she distinguished herself at games and music, acting as the leading violinist in the school orchestra and winning the singing prize year after year.

Deciding to make a career in music, she proceeded to the Sydney Conservatory, taking the violin as her principal subject and singing as the second, but these were soon to be reversed, for she was involved in a car accident that damaged her left hand slightly and made it impossible for her to manipulate the fingerboard of her violin with the agility required of a professional solo violinist. Nevertheless, she continued to play the instrument and became a useful member of the Philharmonic and Conservatory orchestras for several years.

Sport was already playing an important part in her life, for at fifteen she won the Junior Golf Championship of New South Wales, and while she was at the Conservatory she was chosen to represent Australia in the first overseas team sent abroad. For three years she held the lowest women's handicap in Australia, and on three occasions won the State Championship. This was in addition to winning various awards as a swimmer and in "Grade A" tennis and squash!

Concentrating upon singing, she made her début at a Sydney orchestral concert in May 1931 and was signed-up almost immediately afterwards for a series of broadcasts and tours in Australia and New Zealand. At the same time she was asked to write on sporting

Ibbs & Tillett

Keith Falkner

PLATE XVI

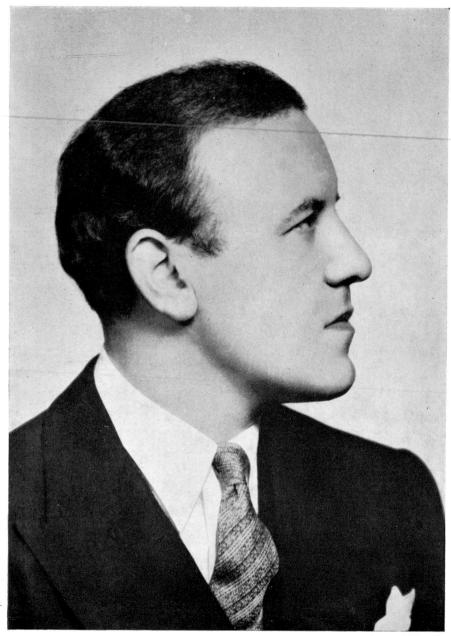

Cannons of Holywood

Eric Greene

PLATE XVII

Angus McBean

Sylvia Fisher as Marschallin
in *Der Rosenkavalier*

PLATE XVIII

Studio Briggs

Joan Hammond

PLATE XIX

topics for several papers, notably the *Sydney Mail* and later the *Daily Telegraph*. She covered the important golfing events, swimming championships, hockey, tennis, squash and net-ball.

What a busy life she must have had in those days! Singing practice and engagements, participation in and reporting of dozens of sporting events, and in 1932 membership of an Italian Opera Company that was touring Australasia at that time. She played many small parts and understudied the principals of this company for several months. No wonder her journalistic work had to be done in the evenings!

Throughout this activity, singing remained her chief interest and the vehicle of her ambition, but she was undecided upon the course she should adopt in order to rise to international reputation until she was heard by Lady Gowrie, wife of the Governor-General of Australia. Lady Gowrie expressed a wish that she should be sent abroad for training, and it was through her influence that Miss Hammond came to Europe to study.

In 1936 Joan Hammond began a three-year course in singing, including opera and languages, on the continent; chiefly in Austria and Italy. Two years later she made her début in London in a performance of the *Messiah* under Sir Thomas Beecham, and in 1939 made her first important operatic appearance in Vienna. In the same year, she came to England to sing for Sir Henry Wood on the opening night of the promenade season, and was in this country when war broke out.

During the war years she served as an ambulance driver in London's East End and on many occasions during the "blitz" she was out all night driving among the shattered buildings. She was on duty during some of the worst raids—on the night when the London Hospital was hit, for instance. Much time was also spent in giving concerts in air-raid shelters, and many thousands who took refuge in the Underground stations will recall her cheering performances. Frequently she sang at the lunchtime concerts held at the National Gallery and the Royal Exchange. Then, when her duties enabled her to leave the capital for a few days, she paid short visits to service camps in various parts of the country to entertain men and women of the armed forces, often returning home just in time to report for A.R.P. duty! From time to time she was able to plan longer tours, chiefly in connection with E.N.S.A. and

C.E.M.A., and has happy memories of visiting naval units at Scapa Flow, touring Allied troop stations in Germany as a guest artist with the Sadler's Wells Opera Company, and frequent appearances as guest artist with the Carl Rosa Opera Company.

Since 1945 Miss Hammond's advance has been rapid: she has established herself as one of our foremost singers in oratorio as well as in opera and has sung frequently under all our leading conductors. In 1946 she toured Australia and New Zealand at the invitation of the Australian Broadcasting Commission giving twenty eight concerts at which she sang songs in four different languages.

On her return to London she received another exciting invitation: to sing as guest artist, in May 1947, with the Vienna State Opera, whose administrators had been so impressed by her gramophone records that they wished to offer her a contract. This engagement proved a great success not only for herself, but for British art in general, and she is justly proud of having been the first British artist to sing at the Vienna State Opera since the end of the war. Among the operas in which she played leading rôles so impressively were *Tosca* and *La Traviata* in Italian, and *La Bohème* and *Madam Butterfly* in German. Later in the same year she sang at the London Music Festival under such famous conductors as Otto Klemperer and Manuel Rosenthal.

Another prolonged tour took place later in 1947 when she visited South Africa and sang at an extensive series of recitals and orchestral concerts as well as making numerous broadcasts and appearing in various films. One film that emphasized her sporting accomplishments caused her to become known as "Australia's Golfing Prima Donna".

Miss Hammond's voice has a compass of nearly two-and-a-half octaves, soaring with ease to a top E-flat. A point of interest is that when she started singing she could rarely go above a top G, but with careful practice she has added over half an octave to her voice. She is blessed with the ability to hear her own voice perfectly—a gift less common than many people imagine—and it is probably because of this that she is able to charm her listeners with such a range of expression.

Her repertoire includes about two dozen principal rôles in opera —her favourites being Violetta in *La Traviata*, Tosca, Manon in *Manon Lescaut*, Elsa in *Lohengrin*, and Elizabeth in *Tannhäuser*. In oratorio she is heard to advantage in the Requiems of Verdi and Brahms, the Bach *St. Matthew Passion*, the Beethoven Choral Symphony and Mass in D, *Messiah, Elijah, Samson*, the Dvořák *Stabat Mater*, and the Berlioz *Childhood of Christ*. She also sings all manner of songs, including lieder and the works of modern English composers.

Her advice to singers is to keep the voice well forward but not to *push* it forward: many people are so concerned about making full use of the resonating cavities of the "mask" that they develop a nasal tone that can be very unpleasant. On the other hand, to sing too far back in the throat is the surest way of wrecking your voice! She has found a great deal of interesting reading in Lilli Lehmann's book *How to Sing*, but warns young singers against applying the advice given in this book to themselves without expert guidance. Miss Hammond also advises singers who are using their voices a great deal to visit a throat specialist four times a year.

A complete rest is often the only cure for ailments of the voice, especially the "wobble" that worries so many people, for this is generally caused by overwork or bad singing habits unconsciously acquired.

When on tour she believes in deep breathing of the air of all places visited in order to keep her voice "acclimatized". This rule stood her in good stead particularly in South Africa, where the altitude of the towns varies enormously. A brisk walk before a concert is always beneficial. Climatic conditions are bound to affect most singers, but it is no use worrying about the many changes that one is compelled to endure when touring. Having frequently flown from the clear, strong air or brilliant sunshine of some continental city straight back to the grimy mist of a winter afternoon in London, she has had many opportunites of testing the reaction of the vocal organs to such drastic changes, and she is convinced that one of the worst things one can do is to "coddle up" indoors, especially in some overheated hotel. A Listerine gargle helps to ward off infection.

Miss Hammond feels that young singers should take more interest in poetry, for it is only when one has learnt to appreciate good verse that one can interpret it properly in song. A knowledge of the theoretical side of music is also essential for singers nowadays owing to the greater demands now made upon their musicianship.

Those who aspire to starry heights in opera should make a special effort to get experience abroad: even a few weeks spent in France, Italy and Germany can be helpful in improving one's knowledge not merely of the languages but of the mentality of each nation as reflected in its music.

The smaller continental opera houses offer wonderful opportunities to learn the whole art of opera from A to Z: they provide splendid training for young singers, and a British artist willing to start in the chorus would stand as good a chance of acceptance as anyone else, provided of course that he or she possessed a suitable voice and a fair general knowledge of music. In these opera houses they are often quite willing to teach the language to newcomers who seem really promising. This, Miss Hammond believes, is the ideal training for opera: it is the sort of thing that can be obtained in this country only in London, since none of our provincial cities possesses its own opera house. Abroad, cities the size of Birmingham, Glasgow, Bristol, Manchester, Liverpool and suchlike all have flourishing opera houses that young singers can regard as training grounds. Even the vexed problem of "digs" does not arise on the continent, for people are so keenly interested in opera that singing students have no difficulty in finding lodgings in which they can practise freely, whereas in England the landlady begins to get bitter as soon as you open your mouth!

Miss Hammond, who received the O.B.E. in 1953, is a staunch defender of British culture, but she warns students that in this country the average professional singer has to *fight* his way the whole time. It is not often that a youthful British artist gets the tremendous encouragement and assistance given to promising members of, say, the Vienna State Opera.

A final word of warning to the younger singer: decide your rôles with the utmost consideration for your voice, because it is easy to ruin your future by singing parts that entail strain. It often happens that an ambitious youngster will accept some part quite unsuitable to his voice merely to oblige a manager who, for the moment, cannot find anybody else to take on the job. A few months or years of this sort of thing and his voice is irreparably damaged; then he discovers to his dismay that the manager casts him off like a worn-out glove, not caring two hoots about what is to become of him.

JOAN HAMMOND

Work takes up so much of Miss Hammond's time nowadays that it is surprising to find her still in perfect form on the golf course, or in any of the other recreations she allows herself from time to time. More than that, at her pleasant home she occasionally indulges in yet another hobby: painting. In the past she has done some commendable work in charcoal, oils and water-colours, from which one gathers that she has a passion for painting ships. Her reading is chiefly of poetry and "the superb literature of the Bible."

Roy Henderson

AFTER enjoying a reputation as one of Britain's leading baritones for many years, Roy Henderson is now devoting himself to the art of teaching and has become recognised as one of the few first-class singing teachers we possess.

He was born of Scottish parents in Edinburgh in 1899, but came to England early in life because his father, a prominent Congregational minister, was appointed to a church in Nottingham and later became Principal of Paton College in the same town. He therefore received his education at Nottingham High School, where he eventually became captain of cricket. Although he sang occasionally at school concerts, it was chiefly at sport that he distinguished himself.

On leaving school he went straight into the army, for the Great War was then in progress, and in the Artists' Rifles he became associated with Charles Mott, an excellent singer who was later killed, and who made a deep impression upon the young aspirant. It was through watching Mott that Roy Henderson learned to sing *Simon the Cellarer* which Sir Henry Wood suggested he should give as an encore on the last night of a promenade season in the nineteen-twenties. The piano lid had to be closed as an indication of finality before the audience would cease applauding.

Not until 1920 was Henderson able to commence his studies at the Royal Academy of Music, and he did so on the advice of Robert Radford. He made up for lost time, however, by working extremely hard with Thomas Meux for singing and J. B. McEwen for composition. In passing, it should be said that he made no pretensions to genius for composition, and throughout his career he has written no more than a few songs. While he was still a student a wonderful opportunity came his way: he was suddenly called upon to sing the baritone part in the *Mass of Life* (Delius) at the Queen's Hall for the Royal Philharmonic Society. As most singers know, this is one of the most exacting solo parts in the whole repertoire of choral works, and the offer of this important engagement at the very outset of his career was gratifying indeed, though he was naturally filled with a sense of awe. However, in less than three weeks he prepared the work so thoroughly that he was able to sing this part entirely from memory: a great novelty in those days.

His success was such that he was awarded the coveted Worshipful Company of Musicians' medal as the most distinguished student of the year, and he was "made" as a professional singer overnight—quite literally. This was all very thrilling, but he soon realized that it was not going to be easy to live up to his newly-acquired reputation.

Offers of further engagements came in with almost alarming frequency, and he did his utmost to fulfil them. This was his one great mistake—as he now acknowledges—for it was foolish to try to do so much: he was teaching both in Nottingham and London as well as singing at important concerts and festivals throughout the country. As we shall see later in this chapter, he urges young singers of today not to make the same mistake.

For all that, his reputation grew steadily not only in the concert hall but in the opera house, where he played several favourite rôles with the utmost taste, and as a choral conductor and choir trainer he was soon to achieve eminence. From 1930 until 1937 he was the chorus master of the Nottingham Harmonic Society under Sir Hamilton Harty. (Henderson says that it was called the Sacred Harmonic Society up to the time of his appointment but the committee decided to drop the "Sacred" upon his arrival!) He realizes that he learned a great deal under Harty, and the strong influence of this eminent conductor remains with him to this day. For several years, too, he conducted the Huddersfield Glee and Madrigal Society, the Bournemouth Municipal Choir and the Nottingham Oriana Choir. A noteworthy point is that the Nottingham Oriana Choir is one of the very few choral bodies whose members sing everything from memory. They enjoy a considerable reputation and have made several successful visits to London.

It was at the 1929 Delius Festival under Sir Thomas Beecham that Roy Henderson established himself as one of the world's greatest vocal interpreters of Delius; a fact acknowledged by the composer himself in a signed photograph now in Henderson's possession which bears the inscription: "to the unequalled interpreter of Zarathustra". This was given to him after a performance of the composer's *Mass of Life*.

Henderson's masterly interpretations of *Sea Drift* are well known, but he has also distinguished himself in many works of Vaughan Williams, notably the *Sea Symphony, Dona nobis pacem, Sancta Civitas* and *Five Tudor Portraits*; in Elgar's *Dream of Gerontius, The Kingdom* and *The Apostles*; in the two Bach Passions, and of course in *Elijah* He once sang the *Messiah* in 1923 but vowed never to sing it again: he points out that the *Sea Symphony* and the *Messiah* are poles apart, and one could scarcely hope to excel in both without an exceptional range.

After seasons at Covent Garden in 1928 and 1929, Roy Henderson did little in opera until the first venture at Glyndebourne in 1934. Here, he found his artistic home, as it were, and he is proud of the fact that he sang there on its opening night, appeared every season, and sang on the closing night before the war in 1939. He played such rôles as the Count in *Figaro*, Guglielmo in *Così fan Tutte*, Masetto in *Don Giovanni* and Papageno in *The Magic Flute*, which earned him high commendation from Fritz Busch the conductor. Glyndebourne, Henderson declares, taught him the value of rehearsal and meticulous care over every detail of the music as well as profound respect for the composer. Incidentally, he can be heard in the HMV recording of *Don Giovanni* (ALP 1199-1201).

He has always been a popular broadcaster, and his association with the BBC dates back to 1924. He recalls that he arrived at Broadcasting House very early one morning and proceeded to sing some exercises in the cloakroom, believing himself to be quite alone. After five minutes of scales and breezy arpeggios he was dismayed to hear the sound of a cistern and to see an official emerging from the other end of the room.

"Oh! I'm extremely sorry: I hope I didn't disturb you" he exclaimed in embarrassment.

"On the contrary," the official assured him, "I found it quite helpful".

Roy Henderson took part in the first performance of many works by modern English composers: Vaughan Williams, Dyson, Cyril Scott, Moeran, Arthur Bliss and Patrick Hadley. Later, he specialized more in recitals, and many will recall the fine collection of English songs he sang at the first Edinburgh Festival.

In his younger days he was known as a high baritone, but in recent years his voice has dropped a little, though he can still sing a high G

Angus McBean

Zinka Milanov as La Tosca

PLATE XX

Bruno

Renata Tebaldi

PLATE XXI

Karl Po

Janet Howe

PLATE XXII

comfortably. The pleasant timbre of his voice has always been one of his greatest assets, while his diction, phrasing and style of interpretation leave nothing to be desired. Probably more than anyone else he is associated with the singing of choral works from memory. He has taken the trouble to learn more than twenty sufficiently well to enable him to sing them without a copy before him.

He was appointed a Professor of the Royal Academy of Music in 1940, having been elected a Fellow some eight years previously. Teaching has always appealed strongly to him, and he has frequently delivered lectures on singing and choral music to musical and literary societies as well as schools. One of his private pupils was the late Kathleen Ferrier.

On one occasion when he was lecturing he remarked on the delinquencies of some choral singers whose faces remained expressionless and revealed that they cared little about the music they were singing. It seems that members of a local choral society were in the hall, for one of them was heard to remark: "He'd be surprised what we should do if we got the same fee as he does."

Henderson believes that a new era in singing started with John Coates and some of his more distinguished contemporaries, for it was then that audiences first realized that a great voice was not everything. People began to demand that a singer should show respect for the poet whose words he sang. As a result of this better understanding of the art of song we find today that the singer has to use his brain a great deal more than in the past: he has to sing with proper feeling, he must understand poetry and be a good musician as well. If by his manner he shows that he is not really moved by the song, he can scarcely expect it to have a profound effect upon the audience.

The pupils of Roy Henderson are generally reminded that a song belongs first of all to the poet, for it was his work that inspired the composer to add the music. Therefore it is necessary to seek the character of the poet and to understand his idea. The composer might modify the poem, but if he is a good artist he will not distort the character of it, mentally, spiritually or emotionally. The singer comes last, and it is his place to understand both the poet and the composer, for his voice is the medium of expression through which both of the creators speak. Singing starts with the heart, mind and soul of the singer taking inspiration from the poet and composer.

A song fails entirely in its purpose if the words cannot be heard.

One of the greatest failings that Roy Henderson has noticed in singers is the tendency not to think about the subject of the song. How frequently one hears *Every valley shall be exalted* sung by a man who has never thought for one moment about the meaning of the words! The most important thing in singing is sincerity: the singer must *feel* what he is singing about—love, hate, or whatever the subject may be. "Sincerity is the key of artistic greatness", Henderson declares, and points out that such men as John Coates were the very essence of sincerity.

The singer should always try to *visualize* the subject of the song. If he is singing about a tall ship, for instance, he should have a mental picture of such a vessel before him the whole time. This is always a great help in interpretation.

Similarly, facial expression is important, for nothing irritates a modern audience more than a singer whose features are exactly the same whether he is singing about joy or sorrow, love or hate, beauty or ugliness! Choral societies often fail in this respect. One frequently sees rows of expressionless faces singing the *Hallelujah* chorus! It is possible, merely by watching him, to see whether or not a singer knows his job. If he does, he interprets the poet so thoroughly that he really acts the part: his expressions and even the balance of his body help to tell the story.

The avoidance of monotony in singing is of the utmost importance, and the young singer is reminded that changes in tone colour are rarely indicated by the composer. Here again it is only by understanding the poem that true and effective tone colour can be achieved. Needless to say, when there is a change of mood in the song there should be a definite change of mood in the singer.

Roy Henderson does not agree with those who say that there has been a decline in singing during the past twenty years or so. "Vocalism has deteriorated," he says, "but *singing* has not". At the present time, however, there is a dearth of first-class singing teachers: people who really understand the technique of voice production and control. Too many teachers at the present time are allowing ill-equipped pupils to sing songs in public after half-a-dozen lessons. This is a great mistake, particularly as they so often sing modern songs, because the composers of today expect singers to be well-trained musicians. The average singer does not pay sufficient attention to the technical side of his art. Many of the voices we hear today are not sufficiently controlled, and the hard grind of scales, scales and yet more scales, which Henderson believes to be absolutely essential, is out of fashion. One can even get "letters" for singing at one of the Royal schools without singing a single scale. No wonder we are cursed with "wobblers", Henderson declares.

Being a very up-to-date teacher, he has great faith in making gramophone records of his pupils' efforts, since by hearing themselves on these "play-backs" the pupils can more easily recognize their faults. Many of them have had some unpleasant surprises!

In his delightful music-room, Henderson also has an oscillograph: an extremely sensitive apparatus which, amongst other things, gives a visual record of even the slightest wobble on a sustained note. When it is tuned to a certain note, a perfectly straight horizontal green line appears on the screen. As soon as the note is sung into the microphone, the waves of sound appear like two or three jagged mountains, and if the singer's voice fluctuates in the slightest degree the "mountains" oscillate sharply from side to side. One or two of the singers we get on the wireless sometimes would probably wreck the instrument! Incidentally, Henderson believes that the practising of sustained notes on the vowel "e" is the best method of steadying the voice, but it all depends upon a controlled emission of breath and a fixed focal point of production.

Because of the great part that broadcasting plays in the life of almost every singer of today, Roy Henderson considers that all singing students should be taught microphone technique. The first thing that a newcomer to broadcasting has to remember is that he must on no account shout. Hundreds of BBC engagements are lost because singers persist in the notion that they must sing at full power into the microphone. This is absolutely wrong: half-voice is quite sufficient. Whether we like it or not, broadcasting calls for a special technique, and there is no need whatever to think about volume. A song sung very carefully and beautifully in a restrained voice "goes over" wonderfully well, for any deficiency of power is made up by the BBC engineer. On the other hand, if you roar into the microphone the engineer will either tone you down drastically or make you stand some distance away from the instrument. In either case the song will suffer.

The necessity of acquiring microphone technique makes it all the more important that a young singer should first learn to sing *piano*. It is quite a good plan to spend one's first six months in singing thus: it is beneficial both to the voice and to the neighbours.

Some professional singers hold the opinion that because of the restraints imposed by the microphone, we are in danger of becoming small-voiced singers. Henderson does not agree with this: he believes that singers naturally endowed with large voices would not lose them by restrained singing, and that such voices would always tell in the concert hall.

There is, however, a danger in over-loading the voice, and he urges young singers, especially those who have recently "arrived" and naturally feel eager to make the most of their success, to limit the number of their engagements so that they have sufficient time to rest not only the voice but the whole body and mind, and to accept only the sort of work that is well within their vocal power and range.

Roy Henderson was married in 1926 to Bertha Smyth, who was one of his fellow students at the Academy. They have a son, Alastair Roy, and two daughters, Shirley and Joy.

One day when Alastair was four years old he entered the room in which his father was practising conducting, and was fascinated by gestures he had never seen before. He watched his father waving his arms about vigorously in an effort to infuse spirit into an imaginary choir, and at the end of the work, went up to the music stand, surveyed the score for a moment and then exclaimed: "Daddy, does it say that you can sometimes push a man over?"

Musicians are of course quite used to this sort of thing, but Henderson has never forgotten his first experience of Yorkshire when he appeared as soloist with a small town choral society. As he stepped down from the platform at the end of the performance the conductor—a local musician of modest reputation—approached him, and feeling that he had not done at all badly, Henderson anticipated a few words of congratulation.

"What do you think of the choir?" the stick-waggler asked.

"The choir?" Henderson echoed, "Oh! very good!"

"Aye . . ." the other nodded thoughtfully, "an' I don't mind tellin' ee that we 'ad four basses ready to taak thy part if tha'd conked out."

ROY HENDERSON

Roy Henderson has always been fond of sport. For many years he was a good all-round cricketer, but lately he has indulged chiefly in golf and fishing. Indoors, anything electrical fascinates him, and he has installed dozens of interesting gadgets in his spacious Hampstead residence, a pleasant house whose furnishings reveal that he is a connoisseur of fine period pieces. It is also the home of two rather naughty but affectionate little French poodles—twins.

William Herbert

ANOTHER eminent Australian singer now settled in this country is William Herbert, who was born in Melbourne in 1920. He had a most encouraging musical background: his father was a gifted amateur singer of Welsh origin, his mother a most accomplished pianist, and his brother, who was later to become an excellent baritone in a semi-professional capacity, shared his interest in the art from early childhood.

Even at the tender age of five, William Herbert was taking part in small concerts organised in connection with the church the family attended, and at the age of nine became a chorister at Melbourne Cathedral, where daily choral services are held on much the same lines as those maintained in the majority of the English cathedrals. The organist and choirmaster at that time was Dr. Floyd, a former pupil of Dr. Arnold of Winchester Cathedral, and under the guidance of this capable and zealous musician his interest in singing and music generally flourished throughout his schooldays. His voice did not break in the usual manner: it deepened steadily into an alto and then into a light tenor, and he recalls that he was about seventeen when he first began to sing tenor seriously.

It was also at this age that he left school and entered the town clerk's office in the Heidelberg district of Melbourne, but he continued his singing lessons with Dr. Floyd and made such remarkable progress that at the age of only eighteen he was allowed to sing all the tenor solos in a performance of the *Messiah* given with a full symphony orchestra in Melbourne.

In the following year he was engaged as soloist for a performance of the Bach *St. Matthew Passion*, and his success in this arduous task made him decide to give up his office work and devote himself to a singing career.

At twenty-one he was well established as a professional singer, and knew all the standard oratorios. The Australian Broadcasting Commission gave him a contract for solo work, and for about four years he toured all the States of Australia doing not only recital work but

WILLIAM HERBERT

singing at many concerts given under the direction of various eminent guest conductors.

During this period he became one of the most favoured tenors in Australia for such works as the Bach B-minor Mass, the *St. Matthew Passion* and *The Dream of Gerontius:* works which inspired him at the outset of his career and which still do today. He also did lieder recitals as well as the usual run of concert work; his clear, pleasant tenor voice and sound musicianship winning him friends all over Australia.

In 1947 he came to England and found success here almost as quickly as he had done in Australia. Just at that time there was, of course, rather a shortage of first-class tenors with youth on their side, but it was gratifying, nevertheless, to be received with such enthusiasm. He established himself in the field of oratorio, general concert work and broadcasting, and has kept to this type of work ever since. During the past ten years he has sung at almost all the English festivals, including the Edinburgh, Three Choirs, Norwich and the Leeds Triennial, and has been engaged as a soloist by most of the leading choral societies in the country.

The offer of a concert tour of Australia allowed him to return to his native land for a while in 1950, and since then he has been a frequent visitor to Holland, Germany, Belgium and other countries of Europe. He seems to be a favourite soloist with the Dutch audiences for the Bach Passions, which he invariably sings in German when abroad, and enjoys a considerable reputation in Belgium as an interpreter of Handel.

His views on music are akin to those of so many who work hard year after year to maintain the choral traditions of this country: a profound respect and a very deep affection for all the great oratorios that have inspired us for generations, and he has a special regard for the works of Elgar. He considers *The Dream of Gerontius* and *The Kingdom* to be two of the most inspiring and satisfying oratorios he has ever known, and rejoices to find that all over the country there is a steadily growing interest in all the major works of Elgar. More and more music-lovers are discovering the great depth and eloquence of these works, particularly the two immortal symphonies, in which is enshrined the soul of one of the most inspired Englishmen of his time.

In Australia, too, the affection for the greater choral works is plain to anybody who travels from state to state taking part in the performance of them, indeed the enthusiasm for music generally is strikingly clear throughout the country.

To students of singing William Herbert would say "concentrate on getting a good flow of tone, with a smooth, even line". He always bears in mind Melba's famous remark: "The best singing is the easiest", and believes that there would be fewer ruined voices if more singers took this to heart. A good artist knows instinctively when he or she is singing correctly, and a singing teacher must be able to detect immediately when the pupil is producing the sound properly. As several other eminent singers have said, those who are able to start their singing life in a cathedral choir are indeed fortunate, and he acknowledges readily that he is greatly indebted to Dr. Floyd for all the experience and good training he received at Melbourne Cathedral.

His chief interests, apart from music, are in painting and antiques. He is a great admirer of the old Italian school of painting and has some good examples in his London home. His chief recreations are golf and cricket.

Janet Howe

JANET HOWE was born of Scottish parents in East Ham and was educated at the Ursuline covent school in Forest Gate. She was taught to play the piano, to sing, act and dance, but as a girl her flair appeared to be chiefly for drama, and everybody presumed that she would go on the stage.

Her voice seemed to develop quite suddenly when she was about fourteen years of age and this naturally encouraged her to give more attention to music. She began entering competitions and festivals, and within a surprisingly short time had won over a dozen prizes.

Shortly after her sixteenth birthday she earned the magnificent sum of fifteen shillings in one week from two "engagements": seven-and-sixpence for singing the night's toast at a Wesleyan bazaar and a similar sum for a few songs at the Beckton Gasworks Boilermakers' conversazione! Yet to a little girl straight from school those tiny fees were something quite wonderful. It was indescribably thrilling to feel that one's own voice could earn real money.

Unimportant jobs such as these led in time to engagements with fees measured in guineas instead of shillings; to masonic banquets, for instance, where more influential people heard her charming songs and made a mental note of her name. She could probably have earned a fairly comfortable income had she been prepared to continue doing this sort of work, but she was ambitious, and realizing that she could never climb to the heights of which she was dreaming without expert training, she sat for a Leverhulme Scholarship, which she won, and which took her to the Royal College of Music. She believes that she is the only singer who has gone *into* the College with this award, for it is generally won by existing students.

The years 1935 to 1939 were therefore spent in study, but that certainly does not mean that they were uneventful. When she entered the College, for instance, she decided that she must have a new grand piano, and as her parents were not very well off, she made up her mind to earn the price of the desired instrument. So at the end of her first term she joined a concert party and spent some tiring weeks in going about the country singing songs in their variety programmes. Some people would be inclined to disapprove of this, but to Janet Howe it seemed to be the only sensible way of getting her piano. It is still in her possession and standing up well to the strain of sharing her busy musical life.

Her expenses at the College proved heavier than she had anticipated, so she augmented her income during those years by accepting engagements from time to time and making occasional broadcasts. One or two more scholarships were acquired, and then, as the most promising singing student, she received the Clara Butt award. This handsome grant, a memorial to the famous English contralto, enables its recipient to finish his or her studies abroad. Of course, this is an expensive business; therefore the interest on the capital sum has to accrue for several years before an award can be made. Janet Howe was the first to receive it, a fact of which she has every reason to be proud.

So she went to Milan, and sang to Gino Marinuzzi, who declared that she had a true operatic voice. Before accepting her as a pupil, he sent her to his colleague Francesco Salfi for special coaching. Her excellent progress can be partly explained by the fact that while she was a student at the College she had paid visits to Vienna during her holidays and received lessons from Fritz Lunzer and Walter Stiasny of the State Opera.

Prospects of establishing herself at La Scala were suddenly shattered when war broke out, and she was obliged to return to England. It was very disappointing, but she returned to her studies and commenced the slow process of building up a reputation on the concert platform and in oratorio. E.N.S.A. and C.E.M.A. work took up much of her time, and although opera was then at a low ebb in England, she did not abandon her hopes of starring in this very satisfying fusion of musical and dramatic art.

In the early autumn of 1941, Anatole Fistoulari, an ambitious young conductor who had recently escaped from France, persuaded Mr. Jay Pomeroy to put on Mussorgsky's simple but colourful opera *Sorotchintsi Fair* at the Savoy Theatre. It was successful, and after a provincial tour was brought back to London and produced at the Adelphi. For this second run in London a new Khivria was required, and after giving her an audition, Fistoulari chose Janet Howe for the part. She had but ten days to learn it, but she managed to do so somehow despite the fact that the text was in Russian, and made her first appearance in this rôle without even an orchestral rehearsal. She continued to contribute to the success of this opera until the end of its run.

Then, quite by chance, she came to the notice of the late Sir Henry J. Wood, who had done so much to help promising young artists. He heard her sing and suggested forthwith that she should come to him for regular coaching. Week after week she enjoyed the benefit of his personal guidance, yet he would not hear of accepting a fee from her. She made her début at his promenade concerts with no fewer than three appearances in a single season.

After a great deal of concert work up and down the country she made another venture into the realm of opera when in the autumn of 1946 she was invited to sing as a guest artist with the Carl Rosa Company. Nothing could have pleased her more than their suggestion that she should play the rôle of Carmen, for this was a part that had always appealed strongly to her. She was coached for it by Zelie de Lussan, a well known American-born French singer who has been acknowledged as one of the best Carmens in French opera, and when the time came for her début she played her part with such verve and abandon that she won an ovation. Musically and dramatically, her effort left little to be desired: she even played the castanets herself instead of following the more usual practice of allowing them to be played by a member of the orchestra while she imitated the movements. This success in Glasgow was then repeated in a dozen other important cities of the north, and arrangements were made for her to play one or two more leading parts in future productions by the same company.

It was probably her success in *Carmen* that was responsible for her being chosen to play the part of a Spanish girl in the film made a few years ago at the Ealing Studios: *Sarabande for Dead Lovers.*

In recent years she has been associated with Sadler's Wells and Covent Garden. She played the part of the Duchess Frederica in the first performance of Verdi's *Luisa Miller* to be given at Sadler's Wells and also appeared as Charlotte in *Werther* (Massenet).

Janet Howe was married on 6 August 1947 to George Hancock, a baritone singer at Covent Garden who was one of her contemporaries at the Royal College of Music.

SINGERS OF TODAY

She is an ardent patron of the theatre and also takes an interest in painting, though she confesses that she can do little with a brush herself. Good novels and books on music form the greater part of her library.

Miss Howe is generally regarded as a contralto, but strictly speaking, she is more of a mezzo-soprano. She has two-and-a-half octaves: low G to the high C that many a soprano is proud to reach! She can sing with ease all the rôles that Rossini wrote for her class of voice.

Parry Jones

WHEN he is in a genial mood, Parry Jones can be a tonic to anyone interested in music, for here is a real "character": a man who has been almost everywhere, met nearly everybody and done practically everything; a man who has stood the King of Norway a drink, told more than one critic where he gets off, and probably disseminated more "stories" and limericks than anybody else in clubdom. A rare wit (when he feels like it) and a sound musician.

Because of his typically Welsh name he is always looked upon as a Welshman, but actually he was born just outside the borders of Wales at Blaina, Monmouthshire, in 1891. His forebears were undoubtedly Welsh. He was reared in an atmosphere of music, sport and politics, for his father was a strong personality; a fervent Liberal with a good singing voice and an untiring interest in games.

As a boy, Parry went to a college in Cardiff, belonged to one or two local choirs and took part in various Eisteddfods, but when he left school he had to go into the mines, like most of the other Welsh singers in this book, because his parents were rather poor, and it was not until he was nineteen or twenty that he thought seriously of singing for a living. He was then taking lessons from a competent Welsh teacher, Norman McLeod.

In 1913 he came to London and went to the Royal College of Music, where he studied with Albert Visetti, Thomas Dunhill, C. V. Stanford and Frederick Sewell. While he was in his second year at the College he received the wonderful offer of an engagement to tour America as a ballad singer with a party of musicians. What a chance for a promising young student! They toured all the forty-eight states, Canada and Alaska, enjoying new experiences, meeting a bewildering variety of people and having, on the whole, a very good time. While they were in New York Parry Jones secured a number of small parts at the Metropolitan Opera House, and he was there when *Carmen* was revived. Toscanini, who was conducting, demanded no fewer than forty-one rehearsals! As Parry Jones says, it was some performance!

At the New York Music Club an extremely lavish reception was held in honour of Charles Wakefield Cadman, for one of this eminent American composer's operas was being produced for the first time at the Metropolitan. Parry Jones received an invitation, and will never forget the dazzling assembly of distinguished musical personalities gathered there. He was extremely anxious to hear Caruso, and asked a lady to send a request to the famous Italian tenor. This was done, and the great man sang the Prize Song from *The Mastersingers*, in Italian, accompanied at the piano by Richard Strauss. At the end, Caruso turned to the celebrated composer and exclaimed in English, for all to hear: "If you write no better than you play, you finish!" When Strauss visited England in 1947— over thirty years later—Parry Jones reminded him of this incident, which he recalled clearly.

Parry Jones and his party returned to England in 1915 aboard the ill-fated *Lusitania*. How vividly he remembers the criminal assault upon that famous ship! They were having lunch when the torpedo struck her. It made no more than a heavy thud, and many people did not fully realize its significance at first. Yet the huge ship went down in thirteen or fourteen minutes, with a loss of life that horrified more than half the world. Parry Jones was, of course, one of the 500 survivors.

Back in London, he had a short rest and then returned to the College. It should be said here that he had two other singing teachers beside those at the R.C.M.—Ernesto Colli, with whom he worked in Milan for some time, and John Coates, "a great artist and a splendid teacher".

In 1916 he had an opportunity of singing with the Beecham Opera Company at the Aldwych Theatre, and in the following year, with the D'Oyly Carte Opera Company. Then the war intervened, for he was called up and put in the Royal Artillery.

Upon demobilization he joined the Carl Rosa Opera Company, but in 1922 moved to the British National, which he declares, was the finest opera company he had ever known. He had a "glorious time" with them, and remained a member until their dissolution. From 1924 onwards he sang every year in the International Season at Covent Garden.

In 1929 the Covent Garden Touring Company was formed with John Barbirolli as director of music, and Parry Jones sang with them for three seasons. He has now played principal parts in sixty operas, chiefly in this country of course, though he visited Germany in 1928 when he sang in *Lohengrin* at Cologne with considerable success.

During the early thirties he ventured into the world of films and sang in two productions made at the Shepherd's Bush studios, one of them being a version of *Die Fledermaus*.

So much for opera. He had meanwhile been building up a solid reputation in the concert hall as well, having appeared at most of the leading musical festivals, including the Three Choirs, the Leeds, the Beethoven Centenary in 1927 and the Schubert Centenary in 1928. Well over ninety oratorios appear in his repertoire, and he can claim to have sung for almost every choral society of importance in Great Britain. He has worked with every world-famous conductor from Toscanini downwards, and has appeared at promenade concerts for twenty-six consecutive seasons.

Although he would hesitate to make a definite claim, he believes he has sung in more *premières* than any other English singer, especially in new works of such composers as John Ireland, E. J. Moeran, Peter Warlock, Frank Bridge and Edmund Rubbra.

He sang in the first English performance of Alban Berg's amazing opera *Wozzeck;* of *Mathis der Maler* and *Das Unaufhörliche* (Hindemith); of Busoni's *Doktor Faust,* Falla's *El retablo de maese Pedro, The Kiss* (Smetana) and Humperdinck's *Königskinder.* These are just a few of the many foreign works in his repertoire.

Of his travels in recent years, his tour of South Africa in 1940 aroused a great deal of interest; and since the end of the Second World War he has sung in opera in Germany and made appearances at Copenhagen, Amsterdam and Oslo.

To give a complete summary of Parry Jones's views on singing and music in general would be impossible in the small amount of space available here, but one of his strongest criticisms at the present time is that, to use his own words, "We have too many vocalists and too few singers; and most critics don't seem to know the difference between singing and vocalisation". He declares that the so-called *"bel canto"* was not singing; it was vocalisation. Those who employed this "method" did not worry themselves about the words.

Fashions in singing change, just as they do in clothes, and we now demand a high standard of our singers. The English singer of today is the best equipped in the world; no foreigner would undertake the enormous and diverse repertoire that we expect our singers to possess, yet our own people can hold their own, both as regards voice and musical ability, with any who come from abroad.

All his life Parry Jones has stood up for the rights of the English musician, and his chief complaint today is that there is no proper organization of music in this country. We need a nation-wide administration to give the people the music they want and to make the best of our musical resources, which are a good deal better than many people imagine, and which could be considerably improved. Now that there has been a great revival of interest in opera, every large city should possess its own opera house. Such provincial opera houses would provide wonderful training grounds for our young singers, who have both the voices and the talent waiting to be properly developed. The trouble with us in England is that we do not take the long view in music.

Parry Jones believes that, on the whole, voice production is fairly good in this country. It is useless to make general rules because every singer's throat is different from that of his neighbour. A practice that can be condemned, however, is that of trying to train one's own voice. This is really dangerous.

On the question of eliminating a "break" in the voice, Parry Jones considers that this can only be done effectively in young singers. The secret is: "close your tone over the break to weld the two registers together."

He would remind singing students that once they have learned the fundamentals of their art they have to work out their own salvation in music: by study, observation and thinking. The one great difficulty is that the young musician has not enough time to study nowadays.

Parry Jones married Miss Dorothy Morris, a fellow student at the Royal College of Music, in 1917. For some years she was known in public as a singer, but recently has done no professional work. They have one son.

At one time, Parry Jones was something of a cricketer, but although he still takes a keen interest in that sport, he never plays now. His chief recreation nowadays, he says, is "having one" with his friends.

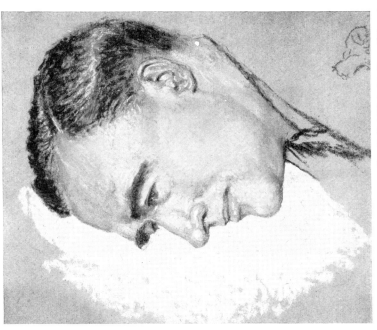

Ibbs & Tillett

Trefor Jones

From the Pastel Portrait by George de Fossard

George Pizzey

Karl Pollak

Roy Henderson

PLATE XXV

This is not strictly correct, for he is a voracious reader. Bernard Shaw once advised him to "read everything that comes along", and it appears that he has never forgotten the famous dramatist's counsel, for his study contains a heterogeneous mass of books on almost every subject under the sun. He has read something or other by almost every living writer and can converse upon subjects far removed from music, though it is rather amusing to find that those subjects so often lead, sooner or later, to politics. (Like most sensible Englishmen, P. J. really enjoys a jolly good grouse about something!) The classics are well represented upon his bookshelves, and he reads a great deal of poetry, believing that it is of the utmost advantage to any singer to possess an understanding and ready appreciation of the poet's art.

9

Trefor Jones

ONE of the most versatile tenors we have in this country today is Trefor Jones, a gifted singer with a rich, clear voice who seems as happy in opera as in oratorio, in musical comedy as in the more sedate atmosphere of the recital hall.

As his name suggests, he is a Welshman, born at Cymmer, near Port Talbot. From his father, a self-taught pianist and organist, he learned to sing a variety of songs at an early age and was encouraged, no doubt, by his mother, who was an excellent singer, but never had an opportunity of using her voice professionally. As a boy, he had a fine soprano voice and sang in many of the local Eisteddfods, at amateur concerts and in various chapels. His first stage experience was gained at a little local performance of a scriptural drama: he was only ten at the time, and played the part of the lion in a scene representing Daniel in the lion's den. Unfortunately it was so hot in the animal's skin that when at the end Daniel put his foot upon the "lion's" head, Trefor Jones fainted.

When he left school he went with most of the other boys of the neighbourhood into the coal mines—really cutting coal at the face —and was not long in discovering the arduous nature of the work. He received an injury to one of his hands that in later years, at the Royal College of Music, compelled him to abandon the piano as a second study. He cannot remember when his voice broke, but when he was about eighteen or nineteen he was doing quite a lot of singing as a tenor in his spare time. He took singing lessons from a local teacher and was determined that sooner or later he would use his voice to get him out of coal-mining.

In 1922 he succeeded in winning an open scholarship to the Royal College of Music where his first singing professor was Gustave Garcia, the octogenarian son of Manuel Garcia II (1805-1906). Trefor Jones spent about four years with this eminent teacher, and still remembers that he was taught to regard his very high notes as pearls: to be treasured with the utmost care and displayed only on special occasions. It was impressed upon him that singing was a life's study. He also studied opera with S. P. Waddington and received a great deal of kindly encouragement from Sir Hugh Allen.

Trefor Jones holds the distinction of having been made the first Hon. R.C.M. in the history of the College. This was the result of a performance of *Parsifal* in which he sang the title rôle under Sir Adrian Boult while still a student. It was an outstanding success, and in recognition of his fine performance, and of the fact that he was an exemplary student, Sir Hugh Allen made this special award.

Another memorable event during his student days was the first performance of Vaughan Williams's opera *Hugh the Drover*. Trefor Jones made such a favourable impression at this *première* at the Parry Memorial Theatre (Royal College of Music) that he was afterwards invited to take part in the Royal Command performance of the opera. At this he was presented to Queen Mary.

Another important engagement to come his way before he left the College was at one of the Three Choirs Festivals at Hereford: he had the honour of appearing as soloist in the *Messiah* beside Robert Radford.

His professional career started immediately he left the College, and he soon found that the English soloist is required to undertake an extraordinary variety of work. Before we proceed, however, it should be mentioned that he returned to the R.C.M. for the Jubilee Performance of *Hugh the Drover*, which was conducted this time by Sir Thomas Beecham.

Oratorio work was his principal activity at first, but several pleasant diversions into lighter fields were enjoyed from time to time. There was a period when he played a principal part in that delightful comic opera *Tantivy Towers* (by A. P. Herbert and the late Thomas Dunhill), for instance, and some years later, Ivor Novello's first big Drury Lane production: *Glamorous Night*, in which he performed a solo part with Novello himself. In 1938 he played the same rôle when the film version was made. Another such diversion was in Herbert Farjeon's *Two Bouquets* at the Ambassadors Theatre, where he took the leading part.

It would, however, be wrong to give the impression that Trefor Jones has specialized in light music, for he sang at most of the Three Choirs Festivals between 1927 and 1939, took part in many of the International Seasons at Covent Garden before the Second World War, did oratorio work all over the country, and made several tours abroad. He recalls that he was broadcasting with the Rotterdam Philharmonic Orchestra from Hilversum at the time of the Munich crisis in 1938, and a little later was touring in Sweden.

He has appeared as soloist at the *première* of several important British works, notably *St. Paul's Voyage to Melita* and *Nebuchadnezzar* (Dyson), and *The Poisoned Kiss* (Vaughan Williams).

As most radio listeners know, he is a veteran broadcaster. His first experience before the microphone was in the very early twenties at Marconi House, which was even before the Savoy Hill days of the BBC. This was when he went with a party of students from the College to illustrate one of Sir Hugh Allen's lectures. He still remembers the heavily blanketed studio and the old-fashioned microphone, which resembled an ancient gramophone horn.

In July 1940 he was singing in France for the allied forces, and was there just before the Germans broke through into Belgium. Shortly after his return to England he registered for military service but was rejected on medical grounds, so he decided to concentrate upon work for E.N.S.A. and C.E.M.A. Much of his singing during the next few years was done in factories, rest centres, camps and so forth, and although he had some fairly exciting experiences in air-raids he cannot be persuaded to talk about them. He can say quite a lot about the miseries of travelling in winter, however, and wonders whether any fellow artist has had a worse experience than a twenty-four hours' delay on Wigan station. This happened one Sunday when he left London at three in the afternoon for Burnley, where he was to sing on the following evening. Owing to a heavy blizzard the train could get no further than Wigan, and he spent the night in the station buffet. When at last the line was cleared it was too late to fulfil this engagement, so he simply had to return to London!

One of the finest audiences he had in wartime was when he sang at the bottom of a coal mine near Nottingham to some three hundred miners. The three items they enjoyed most were the Bach-Gounod *Ave Maria*, Schubert's *Impatience* and Handel's *Art thou troubled?*

In more recent years he has made one or two very successful returns to the theatre, the most important being in the Cochran production of A. P. Herbert's *Big Ben*. He played the leading part throughout its run of nine months.

TREFOR JONES

He always enjoys singing in opera and oratorio. In the former, his ability to act well is an additional asset of considerable value. Dame Ethel Smyth commented upon this some years ago when she wrote in the *Daily Telegraph* that Trefor Jones was the finest Ben she had seen in productions of her opera *The Boatswain's Mate*. This fact also accounts for his popularity whenever he appears as a guest artist at Sadler's Wells. His favourite operatic rôles are Rudolph in *La Bohème*, Julian in *Louise* and Babinsky in *Schwanda the Bagpiper*. In oratorio, he never tires of the great works of Handel, and is particularly fond of *The Dream of Gerontius*, the Bach B minor Mass and Verdi's *Requiem*.

A note should be added here concerning Trefor Jones's many adventures into the world of films. The most interesting, perhaps, was in the first work for the screen in which Anna Neagle appeared, *The Queen's Affair*.

Like one or two other singers in this book, Trefor Jones stresses the importance of singing to an experienced teacher from time to time, even when one has firmly established oneself in music. Quite famous singers have a way of falling into bad habits, and it is only by getting a frank opinion from one who thoroughly understands vocal technique that these habits can be eradicated. For the student, the importance of such a teacher cannot of course be over-emphasized.

Trefor Jones insists that there are no hard and fast rules in singing, for voices are personal instruments with individual peculiarities. Voices do, however, need continual "nursing" if they are to be kept in good form.

With regard to the so-called decline in choral singing, he is pleased to notice a definite improvement all over the country. The worst deterrent now is the unheated concert or rehearsal hall that one finds all too frequently. One can scarcely expect a choral singer to spend a whole evening rehearsing in a draughty building whose temperature is not far off zero.

Trefor Jones is married to Anya Lincoln, an accomplished pianist and singer, who has frequently appeared with him in *Flotsam's Follies*. They often give recitals together. She has also conducted the choir of six hundred voices at the Girls' Friendly Society rallies at the Albert Hall.

Golf is Trefor Jones's favourite recreation—his handicap is

twelve—but he also enjoys driving his car in the country and visiting the theatre whenever there is a good play to be seen. He never tires of reading the works of Bernard Shaw.

Richard Lewis

HERE is a young English tenor of great promise who made a name for himself in many important continental cities before he became known in London: a somewhat curious fact accounted for by his war service.

He was born of Welsh parents in Manchester on 10 May 1914, and his voice was "discovered" at school by a teacher when he was but twelve years of age. It was therefore trained, and as a boy soprano he entered many competitive festivals and made a couple of broadcasts. In 1930 he competed at fourteen festivals, winning thirteen first prizes and one second, which led to his being invited to record for Parlophone. He passed their recording test satisfactorily but unfortunately caught a cold and discovering that many of his top notes had gone, realized that his voice had begun to "break", though actually in his case the process was more of a steady deepening. So the gramophone records were never made; a great disappointment, but as Dr. Cradog Roberts had said of him: "Here is a born singer," he hoped that his adult voice would be no less useful. During the next four years he did no singing whatever.

At sixteen he left school and went into a cotton manufacturer's office. It was a monotonous job but had one consolation: very often in the afternoons he had little to do, so he was able to make good use of this spare time by pursuing his musical studies—at that time, chiefly harmony, counterpoint and the piano. Evenings were spent in studying with T. W. Evans of Manchester, and at the age of twenty he was able to "come out" as a singer. In 1935 he sat for the Associated Board Intermediate examination, won a distinction and the gold medal; in the following year he gained a distinction in their Advanced examination; and in 1937 he secured yet another distinction and gold medal in the Final, which meant going to St. James's Palace to have the award presented to him by the Duke of Kent.

His desire to pursue the technicalities of music still further took him to Dr. W. A. Barlow of Manchester for additional lessons, and meanwhile he continued to save all he could for the day when he would be able to make a full-time study of his favourite subject. That day came in 1939 when he won a Manchester Education Committee scholarship to the Royal Manchester College of Music; so acting upon the advice of Norman Allin, he gave up his job and turned his attention wholly to music.

At the Royal Manchester College he studied for four terms under Allin and then joined an E.N.S.A. party of musicians who were touring the service camps. He did this for twelve months, then one day he had a pleasant surprise: Norman Allin asked him if he would like to sing for the Carl Rosa Opera Company. Lewis was delighted, and for the next two months he toured the northern counties with this company playing in *Madam Butterfly* and *The Barber of Seville*; a pleasant experience brought to an abrupt end by the arrival of his calling-up papers.

He found himself in the Royal Corps of Signals and there is not much of interest to record until 1944 when he went to Normandy with the 21st Army Group H.Q. and was eventually stationed in Brussels for nine months. Nothing could have pleased him more, for he was able to explore this fascinating city, to meet many interesting musical personalities and even to sing at the Conservatoire. He gave a recital there which was attended by Queen Elizabeth of the Belgians with many other distinguished personages, and he was presented to the Queen, who accepted from him a bouquet of blue orchids.

Lewis was engaged by the Brussels Philharmonic Society to sing the solo part in the first Belgian performance of Benjamin Britten's *Les Illuminations*, but alas! he was posted to Norway a week before the concert. However, the Oslo Philharmonic sent him an invitation for the same work, which he performed in November 1945; and in addition he was able to give a recital in the Norwegian capital which was so successful that he was asked to repeat it for the benefit of all who had been unable to obtain seats.

He was still in Norway when the Brussels Philharmonic sent a request to his Commanding Officer that he should be allowed to visit Brussels again to take part in a performance of the *Messiah* and the Bach *Magnificat*. This was agreed, and he was flown to Belgium specially for this purpose in an army transport 'plane. He then repeated these two works at Antwerp.

Following this he had his first home leave for eighteen months, then after a further short period of service in Norway he was posted to Germany in the welfare section at the B.A.O.R. headquarters. Here, permission to accept musical engagements was generously given, and he was able to visit Copenhagen to sing with the State Radio Orchestra under Erik Tuxen and to make quite a number of broadcasts from Hamburg.

Some idea of the impression he had made during the past year or so may be gained from the fact that after his demobilization in September 1946 he was invited to make another tour of Norway. This time he went as a civilian and gave twenty-two concerts in various cities and towns as well as a broadcast of Britten's *Serenade* for the Swedish Radio.

Home in Manchester again, he had to start grappling with the problems of establishing himself as a professional singer and the difficulties of civilian life generally, for in 1943 he had married a smart young "Waaf" named Mary Lingard, daughter of Joseph Lingard, Professor of the flute at the Royal Manchester College of Music and one of the Hallé Orchestra's oldest members.

In January 1947 they decided that they would have to move to London owing to the centralization of much of this country's musical activities, and that brought them up against the problem of the housing shortage. When they first came to town they had to pay £5 a week for a single room in Hampstead! This, with the high cost of living and other heavy expenses did not give them an easy start.

Lewis's first concert engagement came in the same month when he was invited to sing the Britten *Serenade* with the Brighton Philharmonic under Herbert Menges. Then the British Council asked him to take part in a concert at the Hague at which he sang a group of English songs before a distinguished audience including Princess Juliana (to whom he was presented) and Prince Bernhard.

Realizing that there was still plenty to learn in music, Lewis then asked the Manchester Education Committee if they would transfer the remainder of his scholarship to the Royal Academy of Music as Norman Allin was now a professor there, and they agreed to do so for a year.

Further engagements came in slowly; as, for instance, when he was given the chance of playing the part of the Male Commentator in *The Rape of Lucretia* at Glyndebourne in the summer of that year; a performance that he was able to repeat shortly afterwards at the Hague and, in the autumn, at Covent Garden. This led to an offer from the Covent Garden administrators to sing the title rôle of *Peter Grimes*, which he did in November 1947. A few weeks later he was in Holland at the invitation of the Dutch Handel Society singing the *Messiah* at the famous old church at Narden near Amsterdam, and broadcasting from Hilversum.

Thus began a musical career which during the past ten years has flourished eminently, embracing many of the most arduous tasks in the realms of both opera and oratorio. At Covent Garden he played Tamino in *The Magic Flute* and Alfred in *Traviata*, then in 1951 sang the title rôle of *Idomeneo* (Mozart) at Glyndebourne. 1953 was a busy year with such impersonations as Admète in *Alceste* at Covent Garden, Bacchus in *Ariadne auf Naxos* at Glyndebourne (a most effective characterisation) and a slightly too gentlemanly Tom Rakewell in *The Rake's Progress* at Edinburgh. Noteworthy, too, was his Troilus in Walton's *Troilus and Cressida*, but to give details of all his fine achievements would require more space than is available here. A word should be said about his recordings, however. He gives a fine performance of the tenor solos in the Columbia recordings of the *Messiah*, (33CX1046-8), *Israel in Egypt* (33CX1347-9) of Elgar's immortal *Dream of Gerontius* (33CX 1247-8) and of William Walton's opera *Troilus and Cressida* (33CX 1313). He also takes part in the Oiseau-Lyre recording of the Monteverdi *Vespro della Beata Vergine* (OL 50021-2) and has recorded a recital of songs by John Dowland for London International (TW 91067).

Lewis is a fairly heavy tenor—though scarcely of Wagnerian weight—blessed with a fine quality voice of over two octaves: C to top D. It is a truly dramatic voice well produced and artistically used. His preferences incidentally are for the works of Bach, Handel and Mozart, though he is also interested in contemporary music. He believes that it is very wrong of people to decry modern music when they have not properly studied it, for although there is undoubtedly some bad music being written at the present time, young composers should be encouraged to express themselves in new ways. A new idiom in music which strikes us as ugly and unpleasant at a first hearing may prove to be very expressive when we have learnt to understand it. He has found that a knowledge of harmony is quite indispensable to a singer bent on interpreting modern music.

For the benefit of tenors who might be feeling despondent about their high notes, Lewis would point out that it is only through constant practising that he can sing a top C with ease. He has found it best to exercise the voice on the vowel "e", since "ah", which many people favour, tends to send the voice back in the throat. In his opinion, Italian is a far easier language to sing than English, for it contains nothing guttural and uses far more vowels to continue the vocal line, whereas in English the line is continually being broken by a preponderance of consonants.

He attaches great importance to the singing of a true *legato*, and dislikes the practice of singing groups of quavers or semi-quavers disjointedly in an attempt to be precise about their time-value. Accuracy must be combined with smoothness. Lewis also deplores the clipping of a final "m" or "n". In the word "blossom", for instance, one should sing right through the final "m".

In preparing a new work, he always plays over on the piano not merely his own line, but the full accompaniment, for if one has to leap a difficult interval, say, from the tonic to an augmented sixth, it helps enormously to know the harmony of the chord, and of the progression. A knowledge of harmony is a great advantage in sight-reading.

He is intensely interested in Mozart, by the way. The "Mozart style" appeals strongly to him. He listens to a great deal of non-vocal music—especially orchestral works and chamber music—believing that this is essential if one is to develop a well-proportioned musical outlook. Literature is another of his studies and he is also interested to some extent in painting and sculpture, for he feels that a musician should possess a basic knowledge of the other arts in order to become a good artist. His principal recreation is tennis.

Walter Midgley

TENORS are apt to become so painfully superior when they get towards the top of the ladder that it is a real joy to meet one who found eminence while still in his thirties and yet remains a frank, unaffected Yorkshireman. Sincerity is Walter Midgley's keynote: he cannot endure the sort of person who, as soon as he has established himself professionally, draws a veil across his early days to obscure his humble origin and acquires an Oxford accent to go with his "intellectual" pose. He once heard a man who had suddenly transformed himself from an artisan to an "artist" singing: "Ay heyah yuh callin' meh"—and decided to stick firmly to the Queen's English for the rest of his life.

He was born at Bramley, near Rotherham, son of a professional musician who used to spend much of his time at Scarborough singing tenor and playing the trombone—but not both at once! As a lad he mastered his father's instrument, and in so doing learnt the secret of good breath control. It seems that his excellent soprano voice did not break in the usual manner, but gradually deepened and broadened.

When he left school he became a junior clerk at an iron and steel works in the vicinity but was soon earning more than his weekly wages by fulfilling minor singing engagements in the evenings. At first these musical fees were trifling: he once received seven-and-sixpence for singing the *Messiah* but had to pay out nearly five shillings in fares! On another occasion he sang a little cantata known as *Olivet to Calvary* no fewer than five times in a single day—and by the evening was still only a couple of pounds in pocket!

However, while he was earning only seventeen-and-six a week at the iron and steel works he was able to run a better car than that possessed by one of the directors, a fact that puzzled his employers to such an extent that they wondered whether this affluent young clerk was indulging in a little burglary as a sideline!

Slowly, he improved his connections. Minor engagements gave way to invitations to sing at noteworthy social functions and to appear as soloist at the more important oratorio performances, and in time he was encouraged to consider music as a profession. He realizes now the great value of all that spare-time experience— of singing with "scratch" orchestras, unreliable accompanists and choirs whose enthusiasm was apt to run away with them. Hard work, all of it, but a jolly and profitable way of spending one's leisure hours.

After a period of training with Professor Joseph Lycett of the Sheffield College of Music, Midgley found his way into the theatrical world and discovered that he still possessed a few corners that had to be rubbed off. His first full-time professional engagement was in a variety programme. Being rather a conscientious individual, he went to endless trouble at the band rehearsal to perfect various minor details, but at the performance the orchestra seemed to be quite heedless of these matters, so after the show he spoke to the conductor about it. The musical director replied casually: "Oh, that was a different band you were rehearsing with."

More such eye-opening experiences were to follow as he made his way in the precarious world of song, but it takes a great deal to get a keen Yorkshireman down and in due course he was invited to join the Carl Rosa Opera Company. He accepted, started in the chorus, and realized that touring with an opera company was far from being a soft job. The work itself was pleasant, but the conditions. . .! Midgley could tell some grim stories about theatrical "digs". He recalls that in a certain town he was one of five members of the company who had to share a single attic that had evidently been designed by some Victorian architect with a violent grudge against the scullery-maid for whom it was obviously intended.

Still, Midgley learnt his job; just as he learnt the art of singing in oratorio by struggling with little choral societies in the back of beyond. The Carl Rosa Company, despite all the vicissitudes of its chequered career, has always tried to do the right thing, and Midgley's outstanding ability was soon recognized. He began taking principal parts, and these, in turn, brought him invitations to appear as a guest artist with the Sadler's Wells Company, for whom he played the leading tenor rôles in such operas as *The Barber of Seville*, *La Bohème* and *Cavalleria Rusticana*.

At the same time, he was rising rapidly as an oratorio singer and also making some impressive appearances in prominent productions of such musical shows as *The Desert Song, Vagabond King* and *The Student Prince*. Wider experience in time led him to Covent Garden, where·he earned the distinction of being the first English tenor to sing the important rôle of Calaf in *Turandot*. Thus he "arrived" as one of Britain's few leading operatic tenors, a fact confirmed by his engagement for the International Season at the Royal Opera House.

Walter Midgley's recordings include Liszt's *Psalm* 13 on a stereophonic tape for Columbia (bta 106).

Midgley has a superb voice with a compass of approximately two-and-a-quarter octaves up to top D, and is well known for his excellent diction. He is strongly in favour of singing opera to British audiences in their native tongue and fails to see why this should present any great difficulties to a well-trained British singer. It is the duty of every English singer to learn to manipulate the vowels of his language so that his audience can hear the words without straining their ears. He should remember that he is telling a story.

As we have already observed, sincerity is Midgley's "keynote", and he urges all singing students who are striving to become true artists to "sing sincerely, study sincerely, speak sincerely and live sincerely". If a man is not being true to himself, it will surely enough come out in his singing, for his attention cannot be entirely upon his work if he is thinking about posing and impressing people with affectations. There is altogether too much of this "HHwhere e'er you walk" business.

Midgley is not ashamed to admit that in his early days he played the trombone in dance bands for ten shillings a night in order to pay for his singing lessons and he points out that if one or two of our other singers had done likewise they wouldn't be such shockingly incapable sight-readers.

Those singing students who are ambitious to sing in opera should realize that the best way is to start in the chorus, as many of the world's greatest singers have done. So many youngsters nowadays want to skip this "apprenticeship". If there happen to be no chorus vacancies available the next best thing is to get into a musical show of some sort—even a concert party. One can get the "feel" of the stage, become accustomed to singing before footlights and across an orchestra, and acquire a great deal of "theatre sense"

in this way. There is something to be learned in every little part—
even in walking on as a policeman, postman or servant.

As far as voice-production is concerned, any form of oratorio
experience is worth getting, and the greater choral works, especially,
are wonderful singing exercises. If you can sing "Every valley"
from the *Messiah* and "If with all your hearts" from *Elijah* without
any serious fault you are more than half-way towards becoming a
good artist.

Midgley believes that by engaging British singers to sing beside
foreign opera stars of international repute, the present company at
Covent Garden are doing a service to British music, but he is less
enthusiastic about the type of concert promoter who tries to "palm
off" on the public a foreign singer who is almost unknown abroad
but who has come to England in the hope that his foreign name will
make up for his artistic and vocal deficiencies. We ought to do
more to send British artists abroad, because like good cars or other
manufactured articles of quality, they can help to raise our national
prestige.

In criticising the common practice of keeping English singers
strictly to the beat while allowing foreign visitors to have everything their own way, Midgley feels that in opera, conductors should
follow the rule laid down on one occasion by Toscanini. This is
that in ensemble passages, the singers must keep to the beat, but
in all solos the singer should (within reason) set the pace and the
conductor should keep the orchestra accompanying him as a pianist
would on the recital platform. To those who protest that this would
lead to abuses, Midgley replies: "If the singer is not a sufficiently
good musician to be allowed this privilege, he should not be there
at all."

Whenever Walter Midgley is not singing he is generally drinking
tea. His reaction to all the trials and problems of a musical life,
to all the disillusionments, frustrations, irritations and other per-
plexities of today is: "Well, let's have a nice cup of tea!" His wife
says that if she did not keep a strict eye upon him he would make tea
all day long and it is a fact that he frequently gets up in the middle
of the night to make himself a cup. As he neither smokes nor drinks
anything alcoholic, she feels he must be forgiven. He met her before
the war, by the way, when as Gladys Vernon she was working as

pianist in a concert party he joined in the company of Arthur Askey, Jack Warner and Richard Murdoch—fame indeed! They were married in 1939 and now have two children, Walter aged fifteen, and Maryetta aged thirteen. (It is no use arguing with them that Maryetta should be spelt with an "i" instead of a "y"; they simply won't have it.)

Walter is also a goldfish fan, and these piscatorial friends know him so well that they follow him around their enormous aquarium when he makes his daily tour of inspection. Gardening is his chief outdoor recreation, for although he is still interested in football he rarely plays nowadays. He can play a wicked game of billiards and snooker, and believes that Joe Davis is one of the cleverest men on earth.

Of course, being a Yorkshireman he says a lot of things that had better not be put into print, but you can't help liking him. Aye, a great lad is Walter.

PLATE
XXVI

PLATE
XXVII

Left:
Richard
Lewis as
Peter
Grimes
(Angus McBean)

Right:
Kenneth
Neate as
Tamino in
Magic Flute
(Baron)

Parry Jones

PLATE XXVIII

Zinka Milanov

UNTIL her appearance at Covent Garden in 1957, this eminent dramatic soprano was known to music-lovers in Great Britain mainly through the medium of the gramophone, the greater part of her professional life having been spent at the Metropolitan Opera House, New York.

She was born at Zagreb in 1906, daughter of a local bank manager whose surname was Kunc. Her earliest memories are of long, happy days spent in exploring the wonderland of music with her brother, who has always possessed some ability as a composer and pianist. To his accompaniment she sang little songs at home, and at the houses of the family's friends, even before she was old enough to go to school. She always dreamed of herself as an opera singer, and was never happier than when she was performing an excerpt from an opera for the entertainment of the family and friends.

After a conventional education at a high school not far from her home, Zinka Kunc entered the Zagreb Academy of Music to train as an operatic soprano. She was still a student there when she sang at a concert at which the great Wagnerian soprano Milka Ternina was present, and this famous singer was so impressed by the young student's gifts that she offered to train her personally. This expert coaching and the high awards she won at the Academy facilitated her entry into the Jugoslav State Opera, where after taking several minor parts with distinction, she was given the rôle of Leonora in *Il Trovatore* at the age of 21.

For seven years she was a principal soprano with the Jugoslav State Opera, and during this period she commenced her eminently successful tours of European opera houses. She won the approval of Bruno Walter, who engaged her for prominent parts in Hamburg and Vienna.

She began appearing as Zinka Milanov when in 1937 she married Predrag Milanov, a Jugoslav actor and producer who naturally helped her to develop the dramatic side of her art. It was at about

145

this time that she first came to the notice of Toscanini, who engaged her to sing the soprano solos in the Verdi *Requiem* at Salzburg.

As a concert artist she was undoubtedly in the front rank, but she still had some way to go before she could claim to be a mature opera singer. Her début as Leonora in *Il Trovatore* at the Metropolitan Opera House, New York, for instance, was not particularly spectacular. The reason, perhaps, was her unfamiliarity with singing in Italian (she was later to experience some difficulty also in singing in English) but her pure, exquisite tone and sound musicianship sustained her reputation in those arduous days, and within a few months she was able to win the acclamation of even the sourest critics in *Aïda*. There were enthusiastic comments about her rich tone, excellent phrasing and dramatic power, but it seemed that she was still nervous and her intonation was a little faulty at times.

Few who heard her in those days would have predicted such a spectacular rise to fame as she made in the years that lay ahead, but hard work and adherence to sound principles of voice production enabled her to overcome the difficulties that beset her in those early years, and when Toscanini brought her to London for concerts in 1938 and 1939, she was acclaimed as one of the greatest sopranos in the world.

In 1941 she made a tremendously favourable impression at Buenos Aires in the title rôle of Bellini's opera *Norma*: an unusually arduous part, which was later to provide her with one of her greatest triumphs at the Metropolitan Opera House, New York. Curiously enough, this part no longer seems to suit her, for when she sang it at the same opera house during the 1953-4 season, some disappointment was expressed by those who recalled her execution of it eight or ten years previously.

Her rise to fame has not been an easy one: it was not until she had given some really memorable impersonations of such parts as Aïda, Amelia in *The Masked Ball*, Santuzza in *Cavalleria Rusticana*, Donna Anna in *Don Giovanni* and Leonora in *La Forza del Destino* that she was generally regarded as a prima donna. Other notable successes include the name-part in *Turandot*, Madeleine de Coigney in *Andrea Chénier* and Desdemona in *Othello*.

She has few equals as Leonora in *La Forza del Destino*. Describing a New York performance of it in the magazine *Opera*,[1] Mr. J.

[1] June 1953.

ZINKA MILANOV

Hinton Jnr. said that she " . . . blossomed in her full glory, proving again and again that she is one of the supreme exponents of the sweeping Italian line." This is indeed a compliment because one so often hears critics deploring the lack of singers comparable with the great Italian sopranos of bygone days.

Madame Milanov visited London in the summer of 1957. Writing in the *Daily Telegraph*, Martin Cooper declared: "Although the character of *Il Travatore* is predominantly heroic and masculine, it was the women who were outstanding in last night's performance at Covent Garden. Zinka Milanov's refined vocal art and noble conception of the part made her Leonora a revelation of operatic style, and even when her voice lacked the necessary strength and brilliance, the purity and evenness of her tone were exemplary". The same newspaper also contained a lot of gossip about her by a female reporter on the woman's page, from which one learnt that she cannot go out in the rain or in "a nice high wind", cannot smoke, drink, or eat anything cold. "There are, of course, compensations for the privations—such as a lot of diamonds (some of them winked at me), naming your own price for singing, and matching the colour of your car to your dress". We were also informed that Madame Milanov is a friend of Marshall Tito, and that in America she also sings on radio and television: "Not, you understand, on the cheap programmes."

Referring to her performance of the title rôle of *Tosca* at Covent Garden, the *Daily Telegraph* critic wrote: "Zinka Milanov brought to the title rôle a beautiful lyrical quality of tone, a distinction of phrase and a refinement of vocal art which more than made up for a certain lack of power in the big climaxes".

She can be heard in a number of long-playing recordings of operas, including *Il Trovatore* (ALP 1112-3), *Aïda* (ALP 1388-90) and *Cavalleria Rusticana* (ALP 1126-8) as well as a variety of excerpts.

Elsie Morison

LIKE several of the other eminent singers portrayed in this book, Elsie Morison comes from Australia, but it is perhaps interesting to note that she does not attribute to her native climate any particular quality that might be beneficial to good voice production. She believes that a great many Australians sing well because they naturally seem to produce their voices properly, and she has a notion that the accent of most of her fellow countrymen might possibly be conducive to good singing.

She was born at Ballarat, Victoria, in 1924, daughter of Elsie Morison the Australian singer and singing teacher, whose parents migrated from Essex. Her father, of Scottish origin, died when she was a baby. Her sister was a professional pianist for a few years prior to marriage and her brother is an amateur baritone of some merit, so the family was one in which music flourished under the benign guidance of a gifted mother.

Elsie Morison began taking piano lessons at the age of seven, but apart from singing in the church choir with her brother and sister, did little with her voice in childhood. She went to the Clarendon Presbyterian Ladies' College at thirteen, and it was not until she left this school four years later that she began to study singing with her mother. At eighteen she won the Melba Scholarship which took her to the Albert Street Conservatory, Melbourne, where Sylvia Fisher had been a student.

At the Conservatory she studied for three years with Clive Carey and for a year with Harold Browning, finding the dramatic training quite as exciting as the purely musical subjects. She seems to have had little difficulty in establishing herself as a singer in Australia, for she did a variety of broadcasting, recital and oratorio work before she came to England in 1946. Clive Carey had by that time settled in London, so she went to him for a further period of coaching and at the same time taking a two-year course of training for opera at the Royal College of Music, where she eventually won the Queen's Prize.

During this period she had the good fortune to secure her first Albert Hall engagement: she appeared as the soprano soloist in a concert performance of *Acis and Galatea* under the direction of Richard Austin. Mr. Tillett, of Ibbs & Tillett Ltd., happened to be present and was so impressed that he suggested to Sir Malcolm Sargent that she should be engaged for the Albert Hall performance of the *Messiah* in 1949.

She had, in the previous year, joined Sadlers Wells as a principal soprano and was now studying many of the rôles in which she distinguished herself during the next couple of years: Fiordiligi in *Così fan tutte*, Lauretta in *Gianni Schicchi*, Snegourotchka in *Snow Maiden*, Gretel in *Hansel and Gretel*, Nanetta in *Falstaff* and Susanna in *Figaro*.

Her engagements in the field of oratorio, broadcasting and general concert work grew rapidly, and after two years at "the Wells" she resigned to allow herself more time for miscellaneous activities. These included the impersonation of Ann Trulove in the Glyndebourne production of Stravinsky's opera *The Rake's Progress* at the Edinburgh Festival in 1953 and an appearance at Covent Garden as a guest artist in the rôle of Mimi in *La Bohème* in the same year.

Quite apart from the great beauty of her clear and flexible voice, her ability to give a restrained but sincere and convincing interpretation of an operatic rôle made a most favourable impression upon the administrators of Covent Garden, and in 1954 she was invited to become a full member of the company. Her many successes there during the past few years have included Micaela in *Carmen* (1954), Antonia in *The Tales of Hoffmann* (1954), Marenka in *The Bartered Bride* (1955), Pamina in *The Magic Flute* (1956), and Gilda in *Rigoletto* (1957).

In 1955 she also went back to Sadler's Wells as a guest artist to sing the title rôle in the Welsh Opera Company's production of *Menna* (Arwel Hughes), and in the following year she sang Zerlina in *Don Giovanni* at Glyndebourne. Of all these operatic rôles it is difficult to say which proved to be the best vehicle for her particular gifts: perhaps it was Mimi, a part for which she has great sympathy and in which she has few equals at the present time.

Miss Morison has made several very successful tours abroad. Many continental cities have heard her, notably Copenhagen, Paris, Rotterdam and Amsterdam. As in this country, her services are frequently sought as soprano soloist in Bach's *St. Matthew Passion*.

With opera and oratorio taking up the greater part of her time it is not surprising that she has been unable to give as much attention to lieder as she would have liked, yet she has already made something of an impression as an interpreter of Schubert and Schumann, and it is to be hoped that she will expand this side of her repertoire now that she is travelling more. As these words are being written she is about to leave England on a prolonged tour of her native country.

Her voice has a range of about two-and-a-half octaves, possesses a most pleasant timbre and seems able to meet all demands other than those of Wagner. She attributes much to her mother's refusal to allow her to develop her voice until she reached the age of seventeen, and to the very sound training she had in her youth, believing that many a promising voice has been ruined by foolish exploitation at too early an age. One of the most important things to learn in singing is to be absolutely honest with yourself and to know your own limitations. Young singers who try to "burn the candle at both ends" so often overlook the fact that good health is of more importance to the vocalist than to any other class of professional musician.

Elsie Morison has a tremendous admiration for Lotte Lehmann, that superb lieder singer, and for the almost-fabulous Maria Meneghini Callas, whose wonderful stage presence will be remembered long after her lovely voice has faded.

Apart from the fact that she does not sing Wagnerian parts, she has no particular preference for, or antipathy to, any opera or type of opera, but unlike some of the prima donnas of bygone days who took little interest in productions in which they were not personally appearing, she follows the activities of the opera house with the utmost enthusiasm. Incidentally, there are two operas which she would like to see revived: *Louise* (Charpentier) and *Martha* (Flotow). Although neither of them is of importance musically, they are delightfully tuneful and "come to life" well on the stage. The former, which was Charpentier's one outstanding work for the stage, enjoyed widespread popularity at one time because of its depiction of slum life in Paris, which, for some extraordinary reason, never fails in its appeal. It tells of a Montmartre working girl who falls in love with a poet: parental opposition is strong but love, of course, wins in the end.

ELSIE MORISON

When Elsie Morison was a student at the Royal College of Music she met Kenneth Stevenson, the bass singer, who is now a member of the company at the Bonn opera house. They were married in 1950 and at the present time one of their principal difficulties is in trying to arrange to spend a few days together now and then.

Miss Morison can be heard in many long-playing recordings, including John Gay's *Beggar's Opera* (CLP 1052-3 conducted by Sir Malcolm Sargent), Couperin's *Dialogus inter Deum et Hominum* (OL 50079), the Canzonette Opus 4 by J. C. Bach (OL 50132), Arne's *Comus* (OL 50070-1), the Monteverdi *Vespers of 1610* (OL 50021-2), Lully's *Miserere* (DL 53003), and in the following Handel oratorios: *Israel in Egypt* (33CX 1347-8), *Messiah* (33CX 1046-8) and *Solomon* (33CX 1397-8).

Kenneth Neate

WHEN this stimulating young Australian tenor was first introduced to the great audience of British radio listeners in 1945, some people said that Flying Officer Kenneth Neate, as he then was, would make a name in opera on his return to civilian life. As it happened, he had already laid the foundations of such a career in America, so he had no great difficulty in fulfilling this prediction, despite the fact that his years of war service had put him rather out of touch with professional circles.

He was born at Cessnock in the Newcastle district of New South Wales in 1914. His family were all schoolteachers and he originally intended to follow their footsteps, though at school he longed to travel and educate himself by seeing other countries and studying their peoples. He was captain of his high school athletic team and won various championships for jumping, running and swimming.

It was just after he had won a scholarship for University training that he discovered his voice: he heard Giovanni Martinelli singing in one of the early sound films and rushed home burning with enthusiasm to become a great singer. He had for some time been amusing his friends by imitating prominent singers he had heard on the radio, but now it occurred to him that if he had it trained properly, his own voice might be as good as theirs. Moreover, he had already demonstrated his flair for the stage in amateur dramatics, so he joined a local operatic society to test himself in a musical show.

Australia was at that time still feeling the effect of the economic depression of the early "thirties", so it could scarcely have been considered an auspicious time for launching oneself into a new and notoriously precarious profession. Neate was extremely anxious to get to Sydney to continue his musical studies, so he took a job in the police force of that city. For three years he served as a constable, pursuing his studies in his spare time, then in 1939 he met John Brownlee (formerly of Covent Garden and the Metropolitan Opera House, New York) who advised him to go to New York for training.

Neate embarked upon a concert tour of Australia and New Zealand, mainly to convince himself that he had at least a fair chance of making a name as a singer, and then sailed for America in 1940. At New York he placed himself in the hands of Emilio de Gogorza, and after some months of intensive training, was heard by Bruno Walter, who allowed him to understudy Charles Kullman in *The Magic Flute* at the Metropolitan Opera House. This led to his being selected for a series of opera broadcasts by the CBC in 1942, and in April of the same year he had the honour of appearing as a soloist at the Montreal Festival under Sir Thomas Beecham.

Shortly afterwards he joined the Royal Canadian Air Force, in which he was later commissioned as a Pilot Officer, and served as a bombardier until his demobilization in 1946. While he was in hospital with pneumonia in 1943 he had the idea of giving lecture recitals to his fellow airmen, and as soon as he was well enough he started a series of lectures that was to last until the end of his time in the Service.

He came to England with the No. 6 Canadian Bomber Group early in 1945 and was stationed in Yorkshire. Soon after VE-day he appeared in the BBC programme *Atlantic Spotlight* with Bob Hope and Sir Cedric Hardwicke, after which he made several other broadcasts.

On being demobilized he decided to return to New York to resume his musical career, but as soon as he arrived there in May 1946 he heard that David Webster and Karl Rankl were holding auditions for Covent Garden. He applied to them and immediately they heard him they offered him a contract with the new Covent Garden Opera Company. This brought him back to England in the autumn of 1946 to make his début at the Royal Opera House as Don José in *Carmen*. Other parts played by him during that first season were Tamino in *The Magic Flute* and the Singer in *Der Rosenkavalier*. In his second season, 1947-48, he added such rôles as the Duke in *Rigoletto* and Alfred in *Traviata*, which gave him a better opportunity of proving his worth. Later, he has also appeared in television transmissions with equal success, and in January 1948 he made his concert début at the Albert Hall in a Sunday afternoon concert given by the London Philharmonic Orchestra under George Weldon. Being an enterprising young singer he also invaded the film studios.

In more recent years he has spent most of his time singing in opera abroad, especially in Italy, where he has had many successes, including the title rôle in *Lohengrin* at the Rome Opera.

Neate's voice is really quite extraordinary in compass. He has nearly three octaves, from the low F that many baritones call their bottom note up to a top D-flat! He believes that good singing is a science as well as an art, and in order to be a complete master of one's instrument a knowledge of its physiology is essential. Too many teachers, he says, do not understand the fundamentals of correct breathing and vocal emission. We find advocates of abdominal breathing and other systems to which they give fancy names, yet all the great masters of singing, past and present, he declares, adhered to the normal thoracic method.

He has found the practising of *bravura* extremely helpful in enlarging the range of one's voice and maintaining its flexibility. In advising singing students he says: "Practise not only scales and *arpeggios* but long runs from the works of such composers as Handel and Mozart. *Il Seraglio* particularly provides some splendid vocal exercises."

Neate believes that to get a good "ring" into one's singing voice it is essential to cultivate a "free speaking voice". Many British and German singers do not sing freely because their basic speaking voice is tight and not naturally projected into the resonating cavities of the head, he declares, whereas this fault is rarely found among the Latin peoples. Americans are often better than the English because their nasality helps them to keep the voice placed correctly.

To those who are studying to become opera singers, Neate declares: "The mastery of an operatic rôle or, for that matter, any other great musical work, involves months of study and years of development not merely vocally, but intellectually, and should include research into the manners and morals of the period of the subject". For this reason Neate makes a point of calling at the art galleries and libraries of all the countries he visits.

On the subject of opera in English, while acknowledging its desirability, he believes that it is necessary for operatic singers to study their rôles in the original languages in order to gain a better idea of the psychology of the works and a proper perspective of the characters they are impersonating. Another important point is that few translators of opera libretti consider the vowels of the original language in relation to their own translation and the result is that a completely new vocal focus of the vowels is necessary, especially in the higher part of the voice. Because of this, the interchange of languages considerably increases the singer's difficulties. Neate points out that the English language has a greater range of vowel sounds than most other languages, particularly Italian, but at the same time it possesses an extensive vocabulary, so with patient research and diligent application one can find words employing vowel sounds identical with those of the original language, which translate the meaning and at the same time preserve the original vowel sounds. By way of demonstration, he has re-written the text of several arias, and one must admit that the many hours he has spent in so doing are amply justified by the result.

His recreations include the collection—and reading—of autographed biographies, especially those of musical and artistic personalities, and the study—somewhat spasmodically, no doubt—of Vedanta (Hindu philosophy based on ancient scriptures written in a form of Sanskrit).

George Pizzey

AS a specialist in English song and as a soloist in oratorio and secular choral works, George Pizzey has for many years enjoyed a reputation as one who understands the finer points of the English language and who applies this knowledge advantageously in his work. He has proved that the repertoire of a recitalist need not necessarily be based upon lieder, as some people seem to imagine.

The course of his life has been much the same as that of dozens of other singers: choirboy, amateur singer in his youth and then a rather cautious entry into the professional ranks. Born in London in 1898 of parents who were but mildly interested in music, he thought little of the art until he became a chorister at Holy Trinity, Sloane Street, a church famous for its musical services. Here, elaborate settings of the canticles and the Communion service, magnificent anthems, and the infectious enthusiasm of Dr. H. L. Balfour, the organist and choirmaster, fired his interest in music; and when, in time, he discovered that he could reap a great deal of pleasure and a little profit by singing solos very beautifully, he realized that he had "got sump'n", as our American friends would say. Apart from the excellent training he received from Balfour there was also the thrill of being associated with men of the calibre of Robert Radford, who was a soloist at the same church for many years. In passing, it should be said that one of Pizzey's contemporaries was Leslie Woodgate, the present BBC Chorus Master.

The trouble with boy sopranos, of course, is that sooner or later their voices break or "deepen" (otherwise they are apt to become very peculiar gentlemen) and when George Pizzey began talking like a bear with a sore throat he had to face the fact that he would soon be seeking a job instead of the "wings of a dove".

Business life often acts as a spur to those with artistic aspirations: they sit back in their offices, chew their pencils and dream of the time when they will be able to turn their backs upon the vulgarities of commerce and spend the whole of their days in the inspiring atmosphere of their art. (When they eventually get into music,

156

art, drama or letters, as the case may be, they discover that the majority of their fellows have a commercial sense as keen as that possessed by anybody in Throgmorton-street.) George Pizzey was no different from the rest when he went into business, and but for the Great War, during which he served in France, he would probably have become a fully-fledged professional baritone in his early twenties. As it was, he did not commence his studies until after his demobilization in 1919. Then he went first to Robert Greir, father of Arnold Greir, the organist. Later, he had lessons from Frederic King and Eugene Goossens senior, of the Carl Rosa Opera Company, and finally went to Victor Beigal, the teacher of Gervase Elwes and Melchior.

Pizzey soon attracted the attention of various people who had the ability to discriminate between a really promising singer and the dozens of ambitious amateurs who, with passable voices and little else, were on the look-out for pin-money. One of these people, in particular, became a most generous patron to him in those difficult days when he was trying to get a footing in music. Nevertheless, he had to start at the bottom, as it were, and work up. His first few engagements, in 1921, were of the trifling, ill-paid variety that most established professionals would have scorned, but he took them, did them well, and consoled himself with the thought that, if nothing else, they were helping him to "get known".

It was really the BBC that raised him from the obscurity of a suburban singer. His first broadcast was in 1923 from Savoy Hill, and he has many happy memories of those easy-going days before the BBC became a whale of a bureaucracy.

Curiously enough, it was from a humble entertainer who played the castanets (he called them "the bones") that Pizzey originally had the idea of broadcasting. The BBC had but recently been formed—in 1922—and its potentialities were not generally realized. This entertainer heard Pizzey sing at a dinner and assured him that Stanton Jefferies, the original BBC Director of Music, would give him a "date". The youthful baritone therefore applied for this privilege and was booked to give a ballad recital for the princely fee of one guinea. A very modest start, it is true, but one that led to regular engagements on rather more generous terms.

Pizzey often looks back on those early days of broadcasting and recalls with a smile the informal methods of the little staff at Savoy

Hill. He often received an engagement merely through meeting an official on the stairs and accepting a verbal offer made in a few friendly words such as: "Hullo George! I say, can you fill in a quarter-of-an-hour for us tomorrow night?" What a contrast to the oh!-so-dignified official communications one receives nowadays!

In broadcasting during the early and middle "twenties" Pizzey had almost a Jekyll and Hyde existence. Under his own name he would give a serious song recital and then, half-an-hour later, would sing a programme of popular songs under a *nom de plume*.

Now, he is a radio veteran with over thirty years of broadcasting to his credit. He has been "on the air" over five hundred times, and in more recent years has been heard as a soloist in many important broadcasts: of *The Dream of Gerontius*, for instance, of *The Apostles*, *Messiah*, *Five Tudor Portraits*, and Brahms' *Requiem*, to mention only a few. His voice has a compass of well over two octaves: E-flat to G.

But to return for a moment to his earlier days: regular broadcasting did him an enormous service by bringing him plenty of other engagements, but for many years he found it extremely difficult to get more than an occasional assignment in the higher strata of musical activity. He made a "hit" in light opera, and for several years did a great deal of work in this sphere despite the fact that it was not the sort of music that appealed most strongly to him. It was pleasant work, however, and helped to tide him over the years when he was progressing as a soloist from the minor choral societies to the major ones. (Let it be said here emphatically that many of the so-called minor choral societies could teach some of their grander and numerically-superior brethren quite a lot about the art of singing oratorio.)

His first important recital was at the Grotrian Hall in 1927 when he gave an interesting programme devoted exclusively to English songs and won general approval. But oddly enough, it was not until the Second World War that he became recognized as one of our leading baritones: his first appearance at a promenade concert in 1943 being the first of many important successes. Since then he has been engaged as a soloist by the Royal Choral Society, he has sung at the Three Choirs Festivals, and been chosen by Bruno Walter for the solo parts in Brahms' *Requiem*. He was also one of the sixteen artists chosen to take part in the Henry Wood Memorial Concert at the Albert Hall in 1945.

For several years Pizzey did a fair amount of choral conducting in his spare time—as a hobby more than anything else. In this capacity he was associated with two or three choirs in the home counties, and believes that experience of this nature can be most useful to any singer.

Those who experience difficulty in memorizing may be interested to know that George Pizzey never tries to memorize the words and the music together: he has always found it easier to perfect them separately. He also feels very strongly that in oratorio, the dramatic element is apt to be overlooked, or underrated, with the result that the work loses much of its spirit. Those who desire to sing the solos in such works should try to get a proper understanding of the work as a whole—not merely to perfect their own part. They should steep themselves in the "story" of it and feel its atmosphere.

Another little professional tip he has to offer is: "Don't wait for an engagement before you study a score—don't neglect works that suit your voice merely because you think you have little chance of being chosen to sing them." In this simple piece of advice is one of the secrets of his own success. He has always had what is very nearly a collector's mania for buying scores, and he has spent thousands of hours in studying them and learning the baritone solos, even though there seemed to be not the slightest possibility of their being of any use to him. By so doing he has acquired a reputation as a singer who is familiar with lesser-known works and who can often step into the breach when a last-minute illness of one of his colleagues causes a crisis for some concert organizer. On one occasion, for instance, he went to Manchester with Sir Adrian Boult at little more than an hour's notice to sing in the *Five Tudor Portraits*—a work for which he had never before been engaged. It now occupies an important place in his repertoire.

A final word to all lovers of singing, amateur or professional: "Look to the composers of your native land". Far too many splendid songs by English composers are passing into oblivion merely because the average singer will not take the trouble to look for them.

George Pizzey was married in 1946 to Miss Gwen Butteriss, who appears to be filling the rôle of one of his severest critics—musically of course! Of a previous marriage he has two children, a girl and a boy.

To use the words of one of our conductors, he is "a sensible bloke" and heartily dislikes all the "arty" cliques and clans in music. "I like honest-to-God singers", he declares.

At his home at Ashtead, Surrey, he spends much of his spare time in gardening, though he neglects the weeds occasionally for a game of golf, which he plays "after a fashion", or for a day's cycling. Both he and his wife are ardent campers, not of the type who frequent Mr. Butlin's establishments but of that Spartan race who erect flimsy tents in damp fields for the sheer pleasure of catching double pneumonia.

George Pizzey is also a collector of old glass, chiefly Georgian, and china of the old Chinese dynasties.

Constance Shacklock

PLATE XXIX

Cantera

Paolo Silveri

PLATE XXX

Gratton & Douglas

Walter Midgley as Canio in *Pagliacci*

PLATE XXXI

Victoria Sladen

PLATE XXXII

Angus McBean

Maria Meneghini Callas

PLATE XXXIII

Elisabeth Schwarzkopf

ACKNOWLEDGED by music-lovers all over the world to be
one of the greatest German sopranos of our time, Elisabeth Schwarzkopf is particularly well-known in Britain because she spends much
of her time in this country, being the wife of Walter Legge, the
musical *entrepreneur*.

She was born at Jarotschin, in West Poland, in 1915 but is
generally regarded as a German because her family moved to
Berlin when she was a child, and most of her early life was spent in
the German capital. She went to the Berlin Hochschule für Musik,
taking a comprehensive course that included the study of harmony,
counterpoint, history of music, piano and violin in addition to
singing, her principal subject. Her first singing teacher at this institution was Lula Mysz-Gmeiner who unfortunately trained her as a
contralto—not that it did her voice any harm—but this was later
rectified. After two years she became a pupil of Dr. Egenolf. Her
voice developed well under the training of this excellent teacher and
she was soon looking around for a chance to enter the realm of
opera.

When the opportunity did present itself, it came suddenly: she
was given but twenty-four hours' notice to prepare herself for the
part of a Flower Maiden in *Parsifal* at the Charlottenburg Opera
House in Berlin. This is, of course, only a minor part, but not one
that could be undertaken casually for such an important production. However, with Dr. Egenolf's help she was able to master it
quickly and with some trepidation made her début. Everything
went perfectly, and the management was so impressed by her
performance and the promise of her beautiful young voice that she
was engaged as a member of the company: the State Opera.

That was in 1938, and she was soon taking an interesting range of
minor parts which provided her with the experience she required to
undertake principal rôles during the early years of the war. One
of the larger parts she sang was that of Zerbinetta in Richard
Strauss's opera *Ariadne auf Naxos*, and it so happened that Maria

Ivogun, the famous Hungarian soprano who had distinguished herself in this rôle, was in the house. She was quite captivated by Elisabeth Schwarzkopf's voice and immediately offered to train her personally.

Madam Ivogun considered that her sweet, rich voice would enable her to scale new heights as a lieder singer, and she persuaded her to make a special study of this class of work. The glamour of the opera house is always a great temptation to young singers, and the majority, on finding themselves firmly established in it, too often neglect the other branches of their art. Miss Schwarzkopf must therefore be congratulated on taking the older singer's advice: she gave up a great deal of what might otherwise have been leisure time to the study of lieder and in a few years emerged as one of the few really proficient lieder singers of her generation.

An illness checked her advance to some extent, but in 1944 she was engaged as leading soprano of the Vienna State Opera. During her stay of over four years in Vienna she distinguished herself in many rôles, notably Gilda (*Rigoletto*), Rosina (*Barber of Seville*), Mimi (*La Bohème*) and Elvira (*Don Giovanni*), and in the same period she was able to win additional laurels at the Salzburg Festival.

She came to Covent Garden with the Vienna State Opera in 1947, making a great impression here as Elvira. In the following year she joined the Covent Garden company and for three seasons charmed the London audiences in about a dozen leading rôles. The only part that did not seem to suit her was Cho-Cho-San (*Madam Butterfly*), though her singing in this was irreproachable. Her Pamina (*Magic Flute*), Sophie (*Rosenkavalier*), Eva (*Mastersingers*) and Marcellina (*Fidelio*) were perhaps the outstanding achievements.

In 1951 she had the honour of creating the part of Anne Trulove in the première of *The Rake's Progress* (Stravinsky) in Venice, a success repeated soon afterwards at La Scala, Milan. Incidentally at this famous opera house she gave a remarkable performance of Elvira in 1953. Writing in the magazine *Opera*,[1] Peter Dragadze declared: "Schwarzkopf as Elvira was vocally probably almost as perfect as it is possible to be in this part, maintaining a gloriously equal line throughout, combined with superb musicality". Her Elsa (*Lohengrin*), in the same theatre, was sung in the same faultless

[1] April 1953.

162

style, though some critics considered that her voice seemed rather too light for the part.

Her first visit to America was made in 1953, when she gave an impressive lieder recital in New York to stimulate the interest of those who regard themselves as connoisseurs of song. This led to an American tour in the following year, and in 1955 her first operatic appearance on that side of the Atlantic, as Sophie in *Der Rosenkavalier* at San Francisco.

Her artistry received appropriate recognition on October 2nd 1955 when she was presented with the golden Orfeo by Toscanini at Mantua, Italy.

Miss Schwarzkopf is generally at her best in German music—which is what one would expect, of course—she interprets the works of such composers as Beethoven, Brahms, Schubert, Wagner, Schumann and Hugo Wolf with a deep understanding of the composer's purpose. There must be many who recall her fine performance in the Beethoven Mass in D at the Festival Hall, London, with the Huddersfield Choral Society in June 1951.

She seems to have rather a Viennese approach to her art, and it is chiefly in French music that certain subtleties seem to elude her: when she sang Mélisande at La Scala, Milan, many people felt that she was not entirely in sympathy with Debussy's masterpiece of impressionism. It must be admitted, however, that few German singers would have done any better in this opera, in which the composer subordinates everything to the words: the music is almost entirely in a subdued form with mere wisps of motives appearing, vanishing and reappearing, weaving quite a vague harmony.

One would not suggest for a moment that subtlety is a quality generally lacking in Miss Schwarzkopf's artistry: she would not have achieved such distinction in Italian music if that were the case. It should also be said that she has a remarkably versatile voice, capable of a wide range of expression and full of colour.

Her recordings are unusually extensive, embracing many types of music. She can be heard in *Die Fledermaus* (33CX 1309-10), *Figaro* (33CX 1007-9), *Così fan Tutti* (33CX 1262-4), *Hansel and Gretel* (33CX 1096-7), for instance, to mention but a few of the operatic records; she sings in the Bach Mass in B-minor (33CX 1121-3), the Beethoven Ninth Symphony (ALP 1286-7 or 33CX 1391-2) and in the Verdi Requiem (33CX 1195-6).

Her recital records include Schubert lieder (33CX 1040),

Mozart Arias (33CX 1069), Mozart Songs (33CX 1321) and miscellaneous songs and duets. She has also recorded Mozart arias on Columbia stereophonic tapes (bta 103 and btb 302).

Constance Shacklock

CONSTANCE SHACKLOCK is a contralto who seems to have sufficient weight of tone to justify her being cast for even the heaviest of Wagnerian rôles, for she is at her best when singing full-voice and apparently can stand the strain of a whole evening's heavy singing. She has a good compass, too: low F to top C (two-and-a-half octaves), which enables her to sing many mezzo-soprano parts.

She was born on her father's farm in Sherwood Forest in 1913, and her only musical antecedents were on her mother's side. At nine she was singing in the local church choir and a few years later was running a dramatic group at school which undertook chiefly the production of little scriptural plays. But even those modest beginnings "gave her ideas", as people say, and she began dreaming vaguely of becoming an opera singer. She distinctly remembers singing and dancing to a somewhat unresponsive audience of cabbages in one of her father's fields.

The fact that she distinguished herself at music and art (not to mention sport) at school carried little weight with her parents when the question of her future was being considered, for there seemed to be no definite prospects of her being able to use these gifts in a professional capacity, so she was persuaded to go into business. Music therefore became her principal recreation, and during the next few years she received many invitations to sing at church performances of oratorios. Most of her experience up to this time had been gained in the ranks of the Nottingham Harmonic Society, but when it became apparent that people were beginning to regard her as a possible soloist for more important occasions than "musical services", she went to Roy Henderson for lessons and began to study in earnest. She also entered various competitive festivals and won a number of useful prizes.

She always enjoyed concert work, but it never seemed to give her quite the satisfaction she found in being a member of the Nottingham Operatic Society, for here she was given opportunities to use her dramatic talents as well as her voice, especially when she was chosen to play leading parts in their productions of the Gilbert and Sullivan light operas. Consequently, when she began to toy with the idea of taking up music professionally, it was to the operatic stage that she looked for possible openings. But those were the days of Hitler's war of nerves, and nobody seemed to be taking any chances, so for months she hesitated in giving up her commercial career.

In 1939 the question was settled for her by the award of a scholarship to the Royal Academy of Music. She was beginning to enjoy the excitement of planning her future in London as a music student when the war was declared, and her friends all presumed that she would abandon the project. On the contrary, Miss Shacklock went ahead with her preparations, and despite assurances that she was "quite mad", came to town early in that fateful autumn.

At the Academy she became a singing pupil of Frederic Austin, and took elocution and the piano as subsidiary subjects. During the next four years she took all the available prizes for contralto singing, and was twice chosen to appear as soloist at the Academy's annual orchestral concert under the direction of Sir Henry Wood.

Her student days came to an end early in 1944 when she was asked to undertake regular work for C.E.M.A., and the next year or so was spent in touring factories and hospitals with fellow artists to entertain troops and war workers. She could not help noticing the difference between the rapt attention given by the men and women of the forces in the various service hospitals and the rather casual interest displayed by the workers in most of the factories. In such places it was not at all uncommon to find people in the audience reading newspapers, filling in football coupons or playing cards during the performance: in fact they made it fairly clear that what they really wanted was hot jazz from a loudspeaker.

In 1946 Constance Shacklock accepted an engagement with the International Ballet Company to sing in their production of Milton's famous masque *Comus*, and in the summer of that year she was given an audition at Covent Garden, which led to her joining the Covent Garden Opera Company in the early autumn.

Her first year at the Royal Opera House was spent in playing small parts but in the following season she took the title rôle in

CONSTANCE SHACKLOCK

Carmen and played the parts of Azucena in *Trovatore* and Brangäne in *Tristan and Isolde* (the latter in German). At the same time she was also able to accept occasional oratorio engagements and do some broadcasting.

She has a special feeling of affection for Covent Garden because apart from being the theatre in which she established herself as an opera singer it also brought her romance. When she began taking leading parts she had to face the fact that women generally achieve success in opera only by giving up all ideas of marriage until later in life. She decided that the sacrifice would be worth while. Then she was chosen for the part of Brangäne and began working upon it with a young organist who had recently been appointed *répétiteur* at Covent Garden. They soon found that they had much more in common than a love of music, and after a short engagement were married in 1947. His name is Eric Mitchell. This excellent musician with such an engaging personality is one of those kind and sincere people who find it difficult to say a harsh word about anybody. The job of coaching opera singers musically is apt to be a thankless one, for it is seldom that one is given credit for the hours one spends in helping people to learn their parts: one must be satisfied with the gratitude of the singers themselves—if they show it. Incidentally, Mr. Mitchell, who is a Fellow of the Royal College of Organists, is the organist and choirmaster at Christ Church, Gloucester Road.

So the problem of marriage versus career was solved very happily for Constance Shacklock because she works in the same theatre as her husband and shares his interests. But let no one imagine that full-time membership of an opera company is a light job: they spend anything up to twelve hours a day for six days a week at the Opera House, and in addition to a full programme of rehearsals and performances there are dozens of little details that demand attention and which can eat up those odd half-hours in which one has planned to do a little overdue shopping. How do they manage about seeing the butcher and grocer, the window-cleaner, the coalman and all the other tradespeople? It is a mystery, but they *do* enjoy a little home life, all the same. "Occasionally," Miss Shacklock declares, "we get an evening at home, and then we just sit round the fire and say to each other: 'Gosh, isn't it marvellous?' "

Like many of the other Covent Garden people, they lunch together at an excellent but unpretentious little restaurant nearby, but at home, in South Kensington, Miss Shacklock prefers to do her own cooking—and really enjoys it.

On Sundays, she would have every justification for staying in bed half of the day, but she goes to her husband's church both morning and evening like any other dutiful organist's wife. Incidentally, although they are able to visit exhibitions and other theatres only occasionally, they are both interested in painting and "straight" drama. Most of their reading, chiefly biography, is done on the Underground!

Miss Shacklock believes that the preponderance of small voices among English singers is chiefly due to the fact that we so rarely allow our own people to take the heavier rôles. A voice cannot develop on Wagnerian lines unless its owner is given an opportunity of playing Wagnerian parts. In her own case she has found that her voice has developed very considerably both in weight and compass since she began doing larger parts that make a heavier demand upon her vocal powers. She is convinced that in this country we train our singers on too small a compass: limited demands produce limited voices. But she would add a word of warning here: singers should not attempt strenuous Wagnerian rôles until they have passed their twenty-fifth birthday, for in the enthusiasm of youth one can easily put an undue strain upon an immature voice and damage it irreparably.

During the past ten years she has distinguished herself in a variety of operatic rôles, including Amneris in *Aïda*, the title rôles in *Carmen* and *Orfeo*, Octavian in *Der Rosenkavalier*, Delilah in *Samson and Delilah*, Azucena in *Il Trovatore*, Marina in *Boris Godunov*, Queen Elizabeth in *Gloriana*, Brangäne in *Tristan und Isolde*, Fricka in *Das Rheingold* and *Die Walküre*, Waltraute in *Götterdämmerung*, Charlotte in *Werther* (Massenet), Eboli in *Don Carlos*, Adalgise in *Norma*, Venus in *Tannhäuser*, Kundry in *Parsifal* and Ortrud in *Lohengrin*. This is an impressive list considering that she has also undertaken a substantial amount of oratorio work: she has sung the contralto or mezzo-soprano solos in all the oratorios of Elgar, the *Alto Rhapsody* of Brahms, *Das Lied von der Erde* (Mahler), Verdi's *Requiem*, the *St. Matthew* and *St. John Passions* of Bach, as well as in the usual perennials (*Messiah*, *Elijah*, *Stabat Mater*, etc.). Her repertoire also includes many song cycles (Brahms, Bantock, Bliss,

PLATE XXXIV

William Herbert

René Soames

Progress International Press Service

PLATE XXXV

Elsie Morison as Mimi in *La Bohème*

PLATE XXXVI

Hilde Güden

PLATE XXXVII

Norman Walker

PLATE XXXVIII

Houston Rogers

Jennifer Vyvyan

PLATE XXXIX

Britten, Chausson, Schumann and Wagner), lieder of Brahms, Schubert, Wolf and Strauss, and a wide range of French and Russian songs.

It is perhaps interesting to note that she was the first English singer ever to be invited to perform in Russia's famous Bolshoi theatre, and she was also the first English singer to appear in Germany as a soloist after the war. She has sung opera in Amsterdam, Brussells, Paris, Berlin, Buenos Aires and South Africa, and was considered by Erich Kleiber to be the greatest Octavian (*Der Rosenkavalier*) within memory.

She sings in the HMV recording of Gay's *Beggar's Opera* (CLP 1052-3) and in the Nixa recording of the *Messiah* (NLP 907).

Paolo Silveri

ALTHOUGH he stayed in this country for a considerable time during the later nineteen-forties and made a great name for himself in London, this outstanding baritone has in recent years been heard mainly in the opera houses abroad, though some of his recordings are available in Great Britain. Among these we find a recital of Italian songs (seb. 3503) and items from the operas *Prince Igor* and *Carmen* (SCB 107).

He was born on 28 December 1913 at Ofena in the Aquila province of Italy, son of a farmer. As a child he sang and played the harmonium in church, but at ten was sent to a Dominican college near Florence where they hoped to induce him, in later years, to study for the priesthood. Paolo, however, was too fond of the secular life, and on leaving the seminary entered the Italian navy. This proved distasteful to him, and after a few months he managed to secure his discharge.

The next few years were spent in the tailoring business, with singing and boxing as his recreations, until he was called up for the army. By proving to his superiors that he had the ability to organize concerts for his fellow soldiers, he was kept in Turin instead of being sent into the Abyssinian mêlée, for which he was profoundly thankful. But at the end of his period of service his voice was out of condition, and there seemed to be no chance at that time of earning a living with it, which is what he wanted to do. Then he discovered in a monastery the old teacher who had trained his voice in previous years—Perugini—and went to him for lessons.

In due course he was able to proceed to the Academy at Rome, where he won a prize, but unfortunately they persisted in training him as a bass instead of a baritone: he found the singing of deep arias very tiring to his voice.

Then in 1938 he was recalled to the colours, but having recently distinguished himself in a singing competition he was able to persuade the military authorities to allow him short periods of leave

from time to time, so that he could fulfil various singing engagements that were then being offered to him. In the following year,
for instance, he took part (as a bass!) in an important production
of *The Mastersingers*.

When the Allied troops occupied Italy, Silveri found himself a
civilian again and on discovering that his aged singing teacher was
still alive, he went back to him for lessons. The old monk agreed
that he should sing baritone, not bass, and in the period of intensive
training that followed did his best to develop the upper register of
Silveri's voice.

The young singer's first opportunity to take an important baritone rôle came when he was given the part of Old Germont in
La Traviata at the Royal Opera House, Rome, and it so happened
that on the very day he made his début in this opera his old teacher
died.

For the next few months he played minor parts in Rome, then
he went to Naples to join the San Carlos Company, with whom he
visited England for the first time in 1946, making his début here as
Marcel in *La Bohème* and following it up with leading parts in
Tosca, *Pagliacci* and *The Barber of Seville*. He also went with his
company on a tour of Butlin's holiday camps!

On his return to Italy he was engaged for operatic productions
in both Naples and Rome, but came over to England again in the
spring of 1947 to sing at three concerts at the Albert Hall with the
London Symphony Orchestra, conducted by Walter Goehr. These
brought him an invitation to sing for Sir Thomas Beecham and the
London Philharmonic Orchestra and a chance to make a provincial
tour. In Leeds he was asked to give an additional concert because
of the overwhelming demand for admission.

In the summer of 1947 he joined the Covent Garden Opera
Company and sang his first opera with them on 30 August when
they were visiting Glasgow. He sang *Rigoletto* in English, and
believes he was the first Italian baritone to do so. His repertoire in
English now includes *The Masked Ball*, *William Tell* and *Boris
Godunov*, in addition to those already mentioned.

Returning to London after a long tour abroad, he gave a
magnificent performance of the title rôle of *Rigoletto* at Covent
Garden in December 1952. His rich, powerful voice seemed to fill
the house, and at the end of Act II, especially, his vivid sense of

drama gave the audience one of the greatest thrills they had experienced in recent years.

The next few years found him singing in most of the principal opera houses in Europe and also making a very favourable impression at Buenos Aires.

Silveri's voice is resonant and dramatic, particularly in its higher register. He can deliver a tremendous top A, yet descend steadily to a firm bottom G, and throughout its compass his voice seems flexible and colourful.

He practises daily, preferring to do so for a short period before lunch. It is useless, he says, to try to sing early in the morning. He believes that the English do not *throw* their voices sufficiently forward and make too much fuss over their consonants, which are apt to be too harsh for pleasant singing. Singers should practise singing "lovely vowels" and then tack their consonants on to the end of them. To improve the resonance of one's voice he recommends the singing of exercises on "ah".

He has observed many promising voices in England and believes that we could produce some really great singers if only we had more first-rate teachers. The teaching of singing is not, after all, a very complicated art; in fact the old Italian method was simplicity in itself. Singing should be easy and give one pleasure: it should not be regarded as hard work. He is doubtful about the value of reading books on voice production because it is impossible to formulate any definite "method", since all throats are different. One rule he has always kept in mind, however, is that if singing causes undue fatigue it is a sure sign of faulty production.

Silveri believes that we shall get no really satisfactory modern operas until contemporary composers show more consideration for the voice. Many of the people writing operas today do not seem to understand even the fundamentals of singing. We need a few modern operas as singable as *Rigoletto*.

When he first came to this country, Silveri knew not a word of English, but most people will agree that he has mastered the language with remarkable success, and it is significant that he does not regard English as a "hopeless" language for singing; indeed he told the writer recently: "After my own language I like singing in English best."

PAOLO SILVERI

The ease with which he has negotiated the difficulties of our pronunciation is perhaps partly due to his talented wife, Delia Cirino, whom he married in 1941. She is a daughter of one of the finest basses in Italy, he declares, and speaks English fluently.

Both Silveri and his wife are good pianists and are interested in art. They have two children: Juliano and Sylvia, and we are told that the former "has the mouth of a tenor".

Victoria Sladen

VICTORIA SLADEN'S rise from singing in a concert party to taking leading rôles at Covent Garden makes a story of great interest and if the brief details contained in this chapter arouse a desire for further information, this may be found in her own charming book *Singing My Way*.

She was born in Kilburn, London, just before the Great War. There were no musicians in her family, but when she was about four years old a Norwegian singer came to stay with them and aroused her interest in singing. When this lady sang her morning scales, little Victoria, in the next room, would join in and imagine herself a famous prima donna. She had quite a pretty voice as a child but was never allowed to do anything with it, and when she went to school the only way in which she distinguished herself musically was in singing second soprano parts, which none of the other children seemed to be able to do, for they invariably wandered off their line and into the melody. Even in those days Victoria Sladen was a good sight reader.

She was in the middle of her "teens" when her father died, and it became necessary for her to leave school and find a job. Like thousands of other girls, she decided that to do something in an office was the best way of earning a living, so she went to Pitman's College and learned shorthand and typewriting. This, in due course took her into business, but she did not give up her ambition to become a singer: she worked hard at singing and music generally in the evenings and eventually won a singing scholarship to one of the London colleges. This establishment shall not be named because the course there was a great disappointment to her: it got her nowhere. So when she was twenty she decided upon a bold move: she threw up her job and went to study in Berlin.

To anybody in love with music, Germany was an exciting country in those days, and the eighteen months she spent there working under Ernst Grenzebach—teacher of Kipnis—were really illuminating, despite the fact that most of the time was occupied by hard work. She made one or two minor public appearances in Germany and got excellent press notices, which led her to believe that she was on the threshold of a successful career.

Germany was then in the throes of an economic crisis and when the time came for her return to England she discovered that the small amount of money that could be taken out of the country was insufficient to pay her fare back to London. It was all very disconcerting, and she had visions of having to stay in Berlin and scrape up a living somehow. Then she realized that she could wire to her mother and get her to send a return ticket. This she did, and then spent many anxious hours at the airport watching the arrival of 'planes from London. At last, the ticket came, and with a huge sigh of relief she started on her journey home. Germany, she decided, was a splendid place for a period of study, but permanent residence there, with the advent of Herr Hitler, was quite another thing!

Back in London and full of confidence, she gave a recital at the Wigmore Hall and awaited the offers of engagements which, she felt sure, would now start coming in. Did anything happen? Not a thing. Nobody, it seemed, was in need of the services of a good soprano, well trained and quite accomplished musically. Those were, of course, difficult days and many established members of the musical profession were having a lean time, but Miss Sladen had scarcely expected such cold indifference from those who ought to have been willing to do something for a very promising young singer.

She faced the situation very sensibly: it was no use getting depressed, and if one was not wanted at the moment in the concert hall, the only reasonable thing to do was to go where there was a demand. So she laid aside her oratorios and books of lieder for a while and went into variety. Those who provide our lighter forms of musical entertainment were not slow to appreciate her voice, musicianship, personality, and becoming appearance.

The next few years were spent in travelling all over the country in revues and other types of musical shows, operettas and pantomimes. At first, of course, her work took her into some of the most humble of the "smalls", and she has vivid memories of roughing it in outlandish places with every Tom, Dick and Harry in the show business. She will never forget the theatrical "digs" with the brass-knobbed bedsteads and dreary meals. But on the whole, she enjoyed this period of her life: there was plenty of fun and good company, and what is more important, it gave her valuable experience in stagecraft.

Whenever she was in London she made the most of every opportunity to continue her studies, for soon after her return from Germany she became a pupil of Madame Mendl, a fine Viennese teacher who had settled here. Incidentally, she still goes to her for lessons, and believes her to be the finest teacher of singing in the country.

Consequently, when in 1942 she was given a chance to go into opera, she was well-equipped and in perfect form. Her début was as Giulietta in *The Tales of Hoffmann* and as Hélène in *La Belle Hélène* (both works in the same programme) at the Strand Theatre.

At that time she was accepting a considerable number of C.E.M.A. engagements, and it was through her work for this organization that she came into contact with Percy Hemming, who suggested that she should study the title rôle of *Madam Butterfly*. She hesitated at first, for at the moment there seemed little likelihood of being engaged for the part, but on second thoughts adopted his suggestion, with the result that she was invited to sing it for the Sadler's Wells Company at the New Theatre. So successful was she that during the next three or four months she frequently played with them as a guest artist, and then accepted an invitation to join the Company.

As a member of this enterprising group she gained valuable experience of opera and was inevitably brought to the notice of the leading *entrepreneurs*. During the four years she was with "the Wells" she distinguished herself in many leading rôles, notably in *Madam Butterfly*, *Tosca*, *La Bohème*, *Il Tabarro*, *Gianni Schicchi*, *The Bartered Bride* and *Cavalleria Rusticana*.

In 1947 she accepted an invitation to join the Covent Garden Opera Company, and her successes there have included such parts as Octavian in *Der Rosenkavalier*, Pamina in *The Magic Flute*, Eva in *The Mastersingers* and Micaela in *Carmen*.

Having proved herself in the realm of opera, Miss Sladen was offered plenty of concert engagements, but could of course accept only a very limited number. Her first promenade concert was in 1946, and in the same year she sang the soprano solos in the *Elijah* for the Royal Choral Society and took part in the notable broadcast performance of *Tosca*. In 1947 she sang at both the Norwich and

VICTORIA SLADEN

Leeds Festivals under Sir Malcolm Sargent, appeared as soloist in the Royal Choral Society's performance of the Verdi *Requiem*, and was chosen by Sir Thomas Beecham for the part of Brangäne in his memorable broadcast of *Tristan and Isolde*. Not bad for a singer who, a few years previously, "couldn't get a look in!"

Success has not sent Miss Sladen "upstage": she is still "Vicky" to hundreds of her friends and acquaintances in the theatre world and would not have it otherwise. To students of singing and those who are struggling to get a footing in music she says: "Be prepared for an enormous amount of hard work, and don't get downhearted. If you do, remember my difficulties!"

She firmly believes that it is far better to gain experience and make oneself known by starting in the lighter forms of entertainment than to spend one's days in waiting for the opportunity that so seldom comes, or worse still, in seeking "influence". She has never had an influential friend to help her, and has never regretted that fact. There are too many ill-equipped people in music today who are being thrust forward by influential friends. To those who aspire to fame in opera she recommends working one's way up in the Sadler's Wells Company as the best means of achieving one's ambition: there is always an opportunity for the really talented artist at "the Wells".

Miss Sladen's delightfully "liquid" voice has a range of about two-and-a-half octaves from low G, and therefore she is also able to sing mezzo-soprano rôles effectively. Her control of it is exemplary: she can soar to a fortissimo top C without screaming, she can produce a perfect *vibrato* without wobbling all around the note and her range of expression is quite wonderful. She believes in "singing as you speak"; that is, as naturally as possible. In practising scales and exercises she recommends the use of "m" and "n" before vowels to keep the voice well forward.

She finds a glass of port very beneficial to her voice if taken just before she goes on to the stage; hence the tiny bottle that she invariably takes to the opera house whenever she has an important part to sing.

Her memorizing is done "photographically"; in other words, she can visualize the page of the vocal score if at any time she is in doubt about her line: a method that several other singers have found helpful.

René Soames

HERE is another interesting personality: a stimulating character to whom one can apply the description "artist" not merely out of politeness because he is engaged in the musical profession, but because in his own modest way he is trying to contribute something to his art. His light tenor voice is as different from that of the great dramatic tenors as the music of Debussy is from that of Wagner, and like the famous French composer, he seems to delight in using his artistry to make a small amount of material go a long way.

Born of musical parents at Canterbury in 1903, he became immersed in matters musical and ecclesiastical when at the age of nine he won a choral scholarship to Canterbury Cathedral. As in several other English cathedrals, the choristers here were expected to learn the art of playing a musical instrument in their spare time—as if daily services and practices on top of their schooling did not fully occupy their waking hours. (One suspects that this clever little rule was introduced not for the benefit of the boys but merely to save the organist the trouble of teaching them the rudiments of music.) So young Soames acquired a violin, and proceeded to torment the neighbourhood until it was decided that he would be less of a menace on the piano; a happy decision, because he made excellent progress at the latter instrument under the guidance of a local teacher of German origin.

There is no reason to suppose that as a chorister, Soames was any less mischievous than the surpliced imp of tradition; in fact, judging by his waggish propensities at the present time, he must have been something of a handful. However, Dr. C. C. Palmer, the Cathedral organist, was sufficiently impressed by his musical ability to accept him as an articled pupil when his voice broke at fifteen or thereabouts. Throughout the Great War he performed the duties of assistant organist, and by the time he was nineteen he had developed a tenor voice sufficiently good to enable him to go back into the choir, but because of his youth it was ruled that he should be paid a "stipend" of only £100 a year instead of the customary £150.

He recalls that when in due course his remuneration was increased to the latter figure he was obliged to sign a formal contract which guaranteed that if he paid superannuation contributions throughout the remainder of his *forty-one* years of service, he would eventually receive the magnificent pension of £1 a week!

When Soames resolved to make a career as a singer instead of as an organist, the Dean (Dr. G. K. A. Bell, afterwards Bishop of Chichester) allowed him leave of absence one day a week so that he could come to London for regular lessons, a concession for which he has never ceased to be grateful, for he might otherwise have got no further than a cathedral choir.

For eighteen months he studied with Gustave Garcia, who at the end of that period told him that he would never become a singer and advised him to go into business. Having disbursed the whole of his savings on this course of training Soames felt that the eminent teacher might have come to that conclusion at a slightly earlier date. He returned to Canterbury after that final lesson feeling utterly dejected, but being a sensible young man he took his troubles to his fiancée, who consoled him and succeeded in convincing him that perseverance could bring success in music just as it does in most other walks of life. With her help he started to save up again, and he was soon journeying to London once more for lessons: this time with Sydney Coltham, a member of the Westminster Abbey choir, who trained him for about two years and restored his confidence.

Then a vacancy occurred in the choir of St. George's Chapel, Windsor, and as the members of that foundation are provided with quaint little houses within the castle walls, Soames nearly fell over himself in his eagerness to apply for the job, for he and the girl who had proved such a steadfast counsellor were very much in love.

The late Sir Walford Davies, who was then the organist of St. George's, gave Soames an audition, and everything looked very hopeful. He then gave Soames another audition, and things looked still more hopeful. Finally, there was a third audition, after which the youthful tenor and his young lady could almost hear their wedding bells—besides, Christmas was coming! But on Christmas morning Soames received a brief note from Sir Walford, who regretted that he could not offer him the job.

Girl friend once more comes to the rescue of dejected, temperamental young musician. (Somebody ought to make an opera out of this.)

Back to Canterbury, to learn patience on £150 a year. Months of gloom when nothing seems to turn up, when the advertisement columns of *The Musical Times* offer nothing more exciting than jobs in city church choirs at "£20 per annum plus occasional fees." (Somebody ought to write a tragedy about this.)

Then came a little sunshine and hope in the shape of a vacancy at Westminster Abbey for a tenor lay-vicar at £200 a year. Soames applied, got the job and moved to London. That was in 1927, and was the beginning of his climb to the position of a singer of national, instead of local, reputation.

Expenses in London generally prove higher than one anticipates and it was not until 1929 that he was able to marry the girl who had helped and encouraged him: Miss Jane Elizabeth Bird of Fordwich, Canterbury.

Soames stayed at the Abbey until 1937, and then joined the BBC Chorus, which in turn led to membership of the BBC Singers, that excellent little body of singers who set an example to our choirs in psalm- and hymn-singing. While he was at the BBC he made a considerable study of microphone technique, which was to be a great asset when he began his career as a soloist.

At the outbreak of war in 1939 Soames was evacuated to Bristol with the rest of the BBC musical staff, and found himself billeted on a young couple who had been married precisely a week! After experiencing the severe air-raids upon that western city he was moved to Bedford, and it was there that he met Elizabeth Poston, an able pianist and composer of songs, who was to exert a strong influence upon his career, for she taught him to sing the songs of Warlock and to appreciate the works of contemporary composers. They gave many joint recitals of such music.

By 1946 Soames had established himself as a soloist sufficiently to resign his appointment at the BBC, though he continued to be one of the Corporation's most frequent broadcasters. In recent years he has made a speciality of Elizabethan music, for which his cathedral training has so adequately equipped him, and of the works of the French school, a type of music to which he is temperamentally suited. He is also an excellent interpreter of the songs of Peter Warlock who, he says, was a man after his own heart.

René Soames has a compass of about two octaves C to C. His voice is of a pleasant quality throughout, steady and well-produced.

Several of the better critics have commented upon his faultless articulation. His recordings include a recital of English songs in the notable Archive series (epa 37010), a selection of songs by Thomas Campian (AP 13006), and he can also be heard in the Decca recording of the *Tales of Hoffmann* (LXT 2582-4).

His wide experience as a broadcaster enables him to offer useful advice to those who are still apprehensive about singing into the microphone. One of the most important things to remember, he says, is that the microphone picks up a great deal more than many people imagine: it reveals insincere singing, for instance, quite mercilessly.

Even in these enlightened days, many singers seem to forget that the words are just as important as the music, and their singing suggests that they are absorbed in the production of good tone at the expense of everything else. To such singers, Soames would say: "Stop vocalizing; sing the words and don't worry so much about the tone of your voice. If the words really mean something to you they will produce the appropriate tone colour in your voice subconsciously." Too few singers, it seems, understand the psychological approach to singing.

Soames believes that if all singers followed the rule: "Interpret first and sing afterwards," we should get a better standard of singing in this country. He profoundly disagrees with those who declare that English is a language unsuitable for song: he considers it to be the best to sing in.

Many young singers go wrong, he believes, in their choice of songs: they select works whose melodic lines appeal to them, without a thought about the words. Tenors, especially, tend to favour anything that ends on a high B-flat, or offers similar opportunities for vocal display.

English singers would do well to consider the music of their own country first, and to start with the Tudors. Our lovely Elizabethan songs are simple in themselves, but are vocally difficult, and it is absolutely essential that the singer should understand the character of them—of the men who wrote them, and of their social background. In other words, you must get into an Elizabethan frame of mind in order to interpret them properly. It is well to remember that the men of those days were full-blooded individuals with strong emotions. The tranquility of much of our Elizabethan music is of strength at rest, or in relaxation, not the inertia of the effete: there is enough of the latter in more modern music!

Coming to contemporary music, Soames fears that much of it is typical of the age: neurotic, restless and unhappy; and apart from that it is so often lacking in melodic interest.

To those who are thinking of taking up singing as a career he says: "Be prepared to have your heart broken at least two or three times." The possession of a voice is only one of several essentials. The ability to interpret properly, to read at sight, and to speak at least two or three languages, is just as significant.

Interpretation is so important nowadays that it is useless to try to sing a song unless you have had some experience of the subject. If you are going to sing songs of the sea and of ships, you must be prepared to learn something about the sea, to spend time in wandering about harbours in order to get an idea of the atmosphere. Painters don't try to portray things they have never seen; why should a singer? Similarly, you cannot sing pastoral songs properly unless you have some knowledge of country life, unless you have wandered in country lanes, fields and woods and absorbed the character of the rural scene. And if you want to sing about love—try it first!

Young men aspiring to careers as soloists would do well to acquire experience in one of our cathedral choirs, for these ancient foundations provide splendid training in solo and ensemble singing. The repertoire of such choirs usually embraces the music of five centuries, and one becomes acquainted with the movable C clef, with plainsong and the modes, the beauty of the psalter and the delight of good hymn-singing. (Mr. Soames would probably agree that one also meets people with truly incredible notions about themselves, their neighbours and society generally, and the young music student will find the toleration of such people a salutary exercise in self-control.)

We rarely hear good ensemble singing nowadays, and the student is urged to give more attention to this branch of his work. Like the members of a string quartet, one must acquire the art of hearing the other parts as well as one's own, and to "tone in" with them. A good ensemble singer must sink his own personality.

The development of a good "ear" is of course essential in all branches of singing if one is to keep in tune, but a little piece of advice that René Soames offers to those who find themselves getting into difficulties with intonation is: "Watch descending thirds", for these, if carelessly sung, can soon put the singer out of tune.

Finally, he declares: "Try to perfect a sustained tone irrespective of volume. The more concentrated the tone, the further it will travel, and if you have difficulty in getting your voice across to the audience it is well to remember that sound can be focused like a beam of light. Focusing helps to avoid strain and makes one less likely to develop a 'wobble'."

Renata Tebaldi

AFTER hearing her sing the title rôle of *Tosca* at the Scala, Milan, in the spring of 1954, Claudio Sartori declared in the magazine *Opera*:[1] "Renata Tebaldi possesses a voice whose exquisitely suave timbre is enough to console one for the sadness of life, and her artistry numbers among its many qualities perfect placing and rare modulations of tone". This particular magazine, being entirely devoted to the art of opera, does not go in for extravagant praise of singers; on the contrary, one can recall reading some very shrewd and penetrating criticisms in its pages, so a tribute like this is praise indeed.

Renata Tebaldi was born at Pesaro, Italy, not far from Rossini's birthplace, on January 2nd 1922, daughter of Teobaldo Tebaldi, a 'cellist fairly well known in Italian orchestral circles. Music-making at home encouraged her to take piano lessons, and it was with the intention of becoming a pianist that she went to the Arrigo Boito Conservatory at Pesaro. After a few years it became apparent that her voice possessed much more than average possibilities, and when she moved to the Rossini Conservatory at Parma she made singing her principal study, coming under the influence of that eminent soprano Carmen Melis. Later, she completed her studies in Paris under Giusuppe Pais.

Early in 1944 she was obliged to leave Parma because the bombing had become very severe, and in May she obtained her first operatic engagement: to sing the part of Helen of Troy in Boito's *Mefistofele* at Rovigo. Other engagements followed, but she had to wait until the following year for her first resounding success, which was as Desdemona in Verdi's *Otello*. This took her to La Scala, Milan, where she attracted the attention of Toscanini.

At her audition with the famous conductor she sang "La mamma morta" from *Andrea Chénier*. At the end, she was rather surprised when he asked her to sing something else, so she suggested Desdemona's part in the last act of *Otello*. The maestro's enthusiasm

[1] June 1954.

184

Aline Albert

Eva Turner

PLATE XL

Elliott & Fry

Helen Watts

PLATE XLI

was unmistakable: he could scarcely wait for it to finish to exclaim "Brava!, brava!" and he arranged forthwith for her to sing at a special concert in which five of the principals of the Scala were to take part. Thus began her association with the famous opera house whose patrons have witnessed so many of her triumphs.

In Britain we first heard her in 1950 when she came with the Scala company to sing the Verdi Requiem at the Edinburgh Festival, an inspiring performance that was repeated shortly afterwards in London. On this visit she also sang Desdemona at Covent Garden, making a very favourable impression.

Her impersonation of the title rôle of *Adriana Lecouvreur* at the Scala in 1953 was quite sensational: musically and dramatically she was so brilliant that the audience began to cheer before the curtain fell. One of her greatest characterisations in the following year at the Scala was as Tatiana in Tchaikovsky's ever popular *Eugene Onegin*. She sang with remarkable emotion and bearing, and the famous letter song could not have been more beautifully sung.

Similarly, in Rome and Naples she gripped her audiences and within a few years was known throughout the opera houses of Europe. Eventually she was able to extend her fame to America, making her début at San Francisco in the title rôle of *Aïda*: another memorable performance which paved the way for her first appearance at the Metropolitan Opera House, New York. This took place in January 1955, thunderous applause greeting her powerful interpretation of Desdemona, for seldom had this part been sung with such power, richness and emotion.

A week or two later she appeared as Mimi in *La Bohème*. Musically and emotionally her performance left nothing to be desired but many felt that this five-foot-ten soprano was miscast for the part of the "little seamstress".

Then came her vivid portrayal of Maddalena in Giordano's *Andrea Chénier*, and once again she was acclaimed as one of the great prima donnas of the day. The luminosity of her smooth, liquid voice and the manner in which she so realistically entered into the part left an indelible impression upon the memory.

Renata Tebaldi has been described many a time as the greatest Italian soprano of today, and this is probably true, but one would hesitate to describe her voice as perfect: the upper register seems to lack the glorious power and colour of the lower, but that may be due to a desire to dissociate herself from the innumerable operatic

sopranos who scream out top notes as if they were being tortured
with a red-hot poker.

She may be heard in the following long-playing recordings of
operas: *La Bohème* (LXT 2622-3), *Madam Butterfly* (LXT 2638-40),
Manon Lescaut (LXT 2995-7), *Tosca* (LXT 2730-1), *Turandot*
(LXT 5128-30), *Aïda* (LXT 2735-7) *La Forza del Destino* (LXT
5131-4), *Otello* (LXT 5009-11), *Traviata* (LXT 2992-4) and *Il
Trovatore* (LXT 5260-2) as well as in a variety of excerpts, far too
numerous to catalogue here. Her recorded recitals are almost
entirely of arias and other excerpts from operas, which is rather
disappointing because there must be a great many who would like
to hear this glorious singer in other types of vocal music.

Eva Turner

MISS Eva Turner is one of the relatively few English singers who have made a lasting impression in the opera houses of Italy, Germany and America.

She is a native of Oldham, Lancashire, but when she was ten years of age her father was transferred to the south-west of England, where he became head of a cotton concern, and consequently the family settled in Bristol. Here she spent the rest of her girlhood. At school she did exceptionally well in the cookery class, and it was suggested that she should make a career in domestic science; then at a later date it was thought that she might take up languages professionally: but neither course appealed very strongly to her imagination. Some idea of the possibilities of her voice was gained when at thirteen she sang at a Bristol church, but it was not until she heard a concert performance of *The Valkyrie* at the Colston Hall in the same city that she felt the urge to become an opera singer. That was just before the Great War; and a little later, a visit of the Carl Rosa Opera Company, whom she heard in *Il Travatore*, settled the matter once and for all. The opera made such a deep impression upon her that with the least possible delay, she became a pupil of Dan Rootham, a well-known West Country musician who had trained Dame Clara Butt.

Eva Turner was still in her "teens" when she came to London as a student of the Royal Academy of Music, where her training was continued by Edgardo Lèvi. At a somewhat later date she also had instruction from this professor's wife, a well-known teacher of singing, and finally from Professor Richards-Broad.

In 1916 she joined the Carl Rosa Company—the company that had fired her imagination—and began her climb to fame. At first she had only minor rôles to play, but within a few years she was taking principal parts in such operas as *Aïda*, *Turandot*, *Fidelio* and *Cavalleria Rusticana*.

International recognition was soon to come, for in 1924 she was invited to sing at La Scala, Milan. A whole season was spent at this famous opera house under the direction of Toscanini—an experience that she will never forget—then she was engaged by an Italian company that was about to tour Germany. This took her to all the principal cities of that country, where she appeared not only in operatic rôles but on the concert platform. Then she went back to La Scala for a while as guest artist.

The next few years were to see her at her zenith. Her engagements took her all over the world and her name became known in most of the principal opera houses of Italy, Germany and America. In 1927 she toured South America with a company from Milan, and in the following year came back to England to establish herself in the International Season at Covent Garden, making a very favourable impression in *Turandot* and *Aïda*. Having won honours in her own country—which is as difficult for a singer as any prophet—she accepted a three-year contract with the Chicago Civic Opera, an engagement that enabled her to extend her repertoire considerably. This, of course, kept her on the other side of the Atlantic for several months each year, but she was able to return to this country for the International Seasons.

In the early nineteen-thirties we find her in Rome singing *Cavalleria Rusticana* under the composer's personal direction: an experience of social as well as musical interest. Mascagni was noted for his fine suppers after the show, and it was always a great pleasure to be one of his guests. He was a genial soul, and despite the fact that he kept extraordinarily late hours, never seemed jaded or irritable.

The year 1933 found her touring with Sir Thomas Beecham, and in 1935 she was back again at Covent Garden with the same conductor. A point of interest is that in the ensuing year she had the honour of opening the opera season in Turin.

Miss Turner was making several oratorio appearances at this time: she was frequently heard in the Verdi *Requiem* and occasionally in *Elijah*. But opera was her forte, of course, and nothing could have been more appropriate than her engagement for the brilliant Covent Garden International Season in Coronation year, 1937, when she proved once again that England could produce opera singers comparable with any in the world.

After this we find her dividing her time chiefly between America,

EVA TURNER

Italy and London, playing beside singers of the calibre of Gigli in several of the greater operas.

Many a time did she have the honour of singing before royalty, including the late King and Queen, and typical of the sort of notices she received is this report from the *Daily Telegraph*: "Such singing as hers has not been heard since the days of Mme. Destinova —forceful, lyrical, giving to each phrase, to each note, just the warmth, the appeal it needs. Her performance was admirable and the audience which filled the house was not slow to acknowledge it."

When war was declared in 1939, Miss Turner was staying in Italy, as she was to have sung there in the autumn of that year, but she was obliged to cancel her engagements and to make for Geneva, where many other British subjects had gathered to be brought home by special trains. She had been home but a few weeks when, strangely enough, she was allowed to go to Italy again to take part in the opera, for it looked as if Mussolini had made up his mind to keep his country out of the war. She was there until February 1940, and was the last English singer to perform in Italy before that country's entry into the conflict.

It is significant that although she could have taken refuge in any of the ultra-safe localities during the war, Miss Turner chose to remain in London through all those trying years. She made many short tours, of course, chiefly to sing to men and women of the armed forces. After coming through all the ordinary air-raids safely, her home was destroyed by a flying bomb in the afternoon of 3 July 1944. Mercifully, both Miss Turner and her companion had gone out for half-an-hour's fresh air.

On what we still call VE-day (1945) Miss Turner was at the Gaiety Theatre, Dublin, playing the title rôle of *Aïda*. More recently, she has reappeared at Covent Garden in *Turandot*.

Eva Turner's voice has a compass of nearly two-and-a-half octaves; A-flat to D-flat. It is a truly dramatic soprano: even with an orchestra of Wagnerian dimensions she can achieve a thrilling climax, yet her *mezza-voce* is clear and pure, even and flexible. Her voice seems to possess no defined registers, for she can sing a two-octave scale with remarkable smoothness. She believes that most voices can be extended considerably by careful training, and always emphasizes the importance of exercising any sort of voice, whether it be light or heavy, expressly for agility. By maintaining perfect flexibility one can keep all parts of the voice, even the extremes, up to concert pitch. Equally important is practising to develop a really smooth *legato*, and for this she recommends exercises employing long, sweeping phrases on all the vowels.

She believes that the ever-feared "wobble" in a voice, if not caused by nervousness, is the result of strain. It is so often the case that singers who develop this fault have been trying to sing parts beyond their powers. A voice ruthlessly exploited always gives trouble sooner or later.

She also recommends the "photographic" method of memorizing, for her own experience has proved the value of being able to carry in one's mind a visual impression of the score.

A final word of advice to those who hope to follow her footsteps: don't imagine that you can get all the experience you need by singing in a room, otherwise you will find many halls and opera houses quite bewildering acoustically. After preparing an operatic part in a studio one so often finds at the first stage rehearsal that all one's carefully considered graduations of tone have to be abandoned at the last minute, or at least readjusted on the spur of the moment. The student is often in danger of getting too accustomed to the sound of his own voice in a room, which, of course, is nothing like the environment in which the public will hear him.

In commenting on the dearth of first-class young sopranos and contraltos at the present time, Miss Turner declared recently that in her opinion those now entering the singing profession were not applying themselves to the major tasks with sufficient diligence. In the past, a singer would be prepared to spend years in studying and rehearsing just two or three rôles—this was the secret of her own success—but now, the younger singers want to learn half-a-dozen opera parts, build up a great oratorio repertoire, give song recitals, make dozens of broadcasts, dabble in film-work and anything else offering extravagant payment—all in a couple of years! Hence the mediocrity of which we hear so many complaints today.

At one time, Miss Turner generously consented to hear some of the hundreds of ambitious singers who wrote to her for auditions. Very often these people hadn't even bothered to learn properly the notes and marks of expression of the pieces they brought to sing to her! No wonder Miss Turner remarks with a twinkle in her eye: "The young singers of today certainly do not lack self-confidence!"

EVA TURNER

Eva Turner is rather doubtful about the value of possessing the faculty of "absolute pitch"; that is, being able to identify any particular note without reference to a keyboard. This would be a tremendous advantage in sight-reading if music were never transposed, but as transposition is still a common practice, she urges singing students to acquire "relative pitch" instead. The tonic-sol-fa method is useful for this purpose, but Miss Turner considers that the best way is to make a good general study of harmony and counterpoint, for the time so spent will prove a splendid investment in later years. Those who aspire to Wagnerian heights are bound to make a proper study of the theoretical side of music.

At home, Eva Turner delights in a quiet and simple life. Her interest in art is balanced by an equally sincere pursuit of such homely subjects as cookery. Many who have witnessed her triumphs in the greater opera houses would be amused to see her when, in a mood for mental relaxation, she suddenly takes charge of her kitchen and finds a real pleasure in preparing a dish that has just caught her fancy. This is typical of her essentially British nature, which has contributed to her popularity in this country. How different she is from the fussy prima donna of the type who lives permanently in an hotel and who would not put a lump of coal upon her own fire lest it should soil her fingers! Miss Turner's favourite radio programme, by the way, is the Sunday morning service! Out-of-doors, her recreations include swimming and motoring.

Two of her most treasured possessions are a playful pekinese named Yu-Tu and a replica of an exquisite piece of jewellery given to Patti during one of her tours of Russia. It contains fifty large diamonds; one for each of the fifty states of Imperial Russia visited by that great singer of yesterday.

Jennifer Vyvyan

JENNIFER VYVYAN started her musical life as a pianist, then became a contralto and eventually "arrived" as a soprano! Moreover, the process did not take very long, because she was acknowledged as one of our leading singers before she was thirty years of age.

She was born in Broadstairs, Kent, on March 13th 1925. Like most people with the name of Vyvyan, her parents were of Cornish descent, but although singing is supposed to be deeply ingrained in the natives of that Royal Duchy, Miss Vyvyan's father and mother were never very interested in the art. As a child, her enthusiasm was all for the piano, at which she began lessons at the age of five. She was educated at St. Paul's Girls' School, London, which during the war years was evacuated to a variety of other establishments including Wycombe Abbey and Talbot Heath, Bournemouth.

At sixteen she went to the Royal Academy of Music as a piano student, taking singing as her second subject. She acquired her L.R.A.M. as a pianist but her voice responded so well to Miss Pitt-Soper's training that she was able to get a scholarship as a contralto at the same institution. With financial aid from the Academy, for which she will always be most grateful, she was able to make singing her principal study, and thus she came under the influence of Roy Henderson who decided that she should be trained as a soprano. She was already receiving minor engagements as a contralto, but these had to be cancelled so that the upper part of her voice could be developed, and the correctness of Mr. Henderson's decision may be judged from the fact that during the next couple of years she won many prizes at the Academy as a soprano.

On leaving the Academy she was offered a few engagements in Wales, which in turn brought a steady stream of invitations from the Welsh choral societies. Her professional career therefore began in Wales, with oratorio work and several secular concerts: no mean achievement in a country abounding with good voices.

A season in the Glyndebourne chorus enabled her to get the part of Jenny in the English Opera Group's production of Benjamin Britten's *Beggar's Opera*: a success that brought her the mezzo-soprano part of Nancy in the same composer's opera *Albert Herring*. With this company she was then able to make her first journey abroad, a memorable visit to Oslo and Copenhagen.

At the age of twenty-five she won the Boise Foundation Award as a "promising singer" and had the joy of going to Switzerland to study with Fernando Carpi. Lessons every day with this prominent teacher meant hard work but they did not prevent her from enjoying every moment of her stay in that beautiful country.

Her love of opera then took her on a tour of Italy, an illuminating experience because she was able to visit all the opera houses and even to take lessons from some of the *répétiteurs* at the Scala, Milan. How vivid are her memories of that tour! It broadened her musical outlook and taught her much that was to be of the utmost value in the ensuing years.

The year 1950 brought her first Promenade Concert, at which she sang the part of the Wife of Bath in George Dyson's delightful setting of *The Canterbury Pilgrims*. In the following year she went to Geneva and secured the first prize in the International competition.

Engagements were now getting fairly plentiful, invitations to broadcast supplementing the usual type of concert work. In 1952 she sang the part of Donna Anna in *Don Giovanni* at Sadler's Wells and made her first appearance at the Three Choirs Festival singing the soprano solos in *The Messiah*.

The greater part of her work was concerned with oratorio, but in the following year she appeared as Electra in the Glyndebourne production of Mozart's *Idomeneo* at the Edinburgh Festival and in 1954 she played the leading part in the first production of *The Turn of the Screw* (Benjamin Britten) in Venice (recorded by Decca, LXT 5038-9). She was later to appear in this opera in many European countries, including Germany, Holland, Italy and Belgium.

In 1956 she went with Sir Arthur Bliss and his party to the Soviet Union and gave concerts in Moscow, Leningrad, Kiev and Kharkov. When she accepted an invitation to appear on the Russian television programme she imagined that it would be for a half- or three-quarter hour concert of the type we televise in England. To her astonishment it was for a concert lasting two-

and-a-half hours! She discovered that the Russians love these prolonged television concerts.

Jennifer Vyvyan's repertoire embraces music of many periods and types: she does not believe in specialisation, though circumstances have led her mainly into the fields of oratorio and recital work. She has a great affection for Dyson's *Canterbury Pilgrims*, an extremely interesting work that has been unwarrantably neglected.

She deplores "singing into a book" and believes that all professional singers should memorise their repertoire, except in the case of a few works which one could scarcely undertake without a vocal score in hand. A singer has so much to convey, particularly when one is singing in a work such as the *Messiah*, and this cannot be done properly if one's eyes are concentrated upon the book most of the time. Those who have heard her would certainly not accuse Jennifer Vyvyan of singing without feeling, in fact her deeply-felt interpretations have contributed in no small measure to her many successes.

In addition to the opera recording already mentioned, she can be heard in the Decca recording of Britten's *Little Sweep* (LXT 5163) and in the Oiseau-Lyre *Semele* (Handel; OL 50098-10). She takes part in Decca's issue of the *Messiah* (LXT 2921-4) and in the Oiseau-Lyre recording of Six Canzonetti (Opus 4) by J. C. Bach as well as the Mozart *Litaniae de venerabili altaris sacramento* (K.243; OL 50086). To date, she has recorded four recitals: English Songs (lw 5102), Mozart Arias (lw 5247), "Songs of England" (LXT 2797), and "Music of Couperin" (OL 50079).

Norman Walker

LANCASHIRE has given us many first-rate musicians, from Sir Thomas Beecham downwards, and one of the best in the world of song is Norman Walker, a splendid bass who combines a good compass—a substantial bottom D and an easy top F—with a quality that could scarcely offend even the most fastidious critic of the vocal art.

He was born of a musical family at Shaw, near Oldham, in 1907. His father played the trombone in an amateur brass band and his mother, a good soprano, was well known in the district as one who could always be relied upon to "oblige with a song". Norman was a choirboy at the local parish church, and was sufficiently keen on music to study the subject at evening classes when on leaving school he entered a cotton mill. At fifteen-and-a-half he had already developed a resonant bass voice that made him a useful member of the choral class at the evening institute where he was studying harmony, and within two years he had made his first public appearance as a soloist in a programme that included some Handel arias.

Soon after his eighteenth birthday he sang for Mrs. Percy Pitt, wife of the English conductor who died in 1932, and was sent by her to Laurence Lee for a year's training. He was still working in a cotton mill at this time, but making a name locally in amateur productions of Gilbert and Sullivan, the light operas of Edward German and suchlike.

In 1929 he won the Sarah Andrews Scholarship to the Royal Manchester College of Music, where for three years he studied singing under Richard Evans. He left the mill and threw all his energy into his course, playing an important part in the College opera productions—notably *The Magic Flute*—and eventually winning the Curtis Gold Medal.

When his scholarship expired he was keen to come to London, so he sang for Sir Landon Ronald, who awarded him the Heilbut Major Scholarship to the Guildhall School of Music, where he embarked upon a further course of study with Walter Hyde. The enterprising opera class at the Guildhall School provided him with many excellent opportunities, and it was in their production of *Autumn Crocus* that he was heard by Basil Dean, who invited him to make a film test. As a result of this he appeared in such films as *Java Head* with Anna May Wong, *Sing as We Go* with Gracie Fields, and also in the latter's *Look up and Laugh*. Later he sang in the film based on the life of Mozart, *Whom the Gods Love*.

Incidentally, when Walker came to London one or two people impressed upon him that he must be careful not to relax into a Lancashire accent when singing. This advice was taken so seriously that when Basil Dean heard him rehearsing for *Sing as We Go* he commented favourably upon Walker's singing but said that what he *really* wanted for the part was a man with a bit of a Lancashire accent!

Walker's first concert with the Hallé Orchestra and Choir was in 1933, when he sang in the Bach B-minor Mass. This was the first of many important oratorio engagements and was to lead to his being chosen by Sir Thomas Beecham to sing at a performance of the Verdi *Requiem* at the Queen's Hall by the Royal Philharmonic Society in 1935, the year in which he made his first important broadcast and became associated with Covent Garden.

At the Royal Opera House he played only minor parts for the first year or two, but then the more important rôles began to come his way and in 1939 he sang as King Mark in *Tristan*. (He believes he is the only Englishman to have sung this in German at Covent Garden.) In that year he played the part of the King in *Aïda* in a distinguished cast including Gigli.

In 1941 Walker was commissioned in the R.A.F. and served as a Flying Control Officer until his demobilization as a Flight Lieutenant in November 1945. He was of course able to do very little singing in the war years, but it was during that period that he received two Fellowships: of the Royal Manchester College of Music in 1941 and of the Guildhall School of Music in 1945. Since his return to civilian life he has again been heard at Covent Garden, but the greater part of his work has been in oratorio. He has also done a fair amount of lieder singing for the BBC. His oratorio repertoire includes all the major works of Bach, Handel and Elgar, and it is perhaps worth recording that he considers *The Dream of Gerontius* to be one of the finest choral works ever written.

Walker believes that it is the quality of sound produced that is the most important thing in singing today: it is not sufficient to have a big voice and one cannot make headway with merely a large repertoire. He always recalls what his father told him many years ago: "It's not the amount you sing that matters, it's the way you sing what you know."

The worst faults he has observed among the younger singer are lack of style and the inability to sing a true *legato*. "It is important that one should see a musical phrase as a whole: it is like speaking a sentence, and the continuity of breath must be preserved throughout."

One of the principal aims of the singing student should be to produce an even sound throughout the entire range of his voice, and in stressing the necessity of ease, relaxation and naturalness in production, Walker quotes the old rule: "If it is not easy, it is wrong." All the vowel sounds should be used in singing exercises, since all have to be sung in works using the English language, and much can be done during these exercises to produce them with the requisite purity.

Walker insists that there is no such thing as "microphone technique": it is merely a matter of singing one's words distinctly. It is true that the BBC engineers can amplify a small voice and modify an exuberant one, but it is foolish to rely upon them to balance your voice. There is a danger of your voice losing a lot of character if you adopt the practice of singing everything quietly and close to the microphone. In his opinion, the best thing is to sing naturally, as in a concert hall.

In order to achieve good resonance it is well to place the voice so that it feels even higher than "behind the nose". Only by making the most of the resonating cavities can one produce a real *fortissimo*: if you try to get it by any other method you will ruin your voice. It is well to remember, too, that a ringing voice travels much further in the concert hall than one lacking resonance. "But watch the quality all the time: it is dangerous to get too bright a tone because it will quickly become strident."

A final word to the singing student: don't imagine that a good teacher can do everything for you; a great deal of effort is required upon your part. To this Norman Walker would add a remark that Sir Henry Wood made to him some years ago: "The longer it takes you to 'arrive', the longer you will stay."

Helen Watts

ANOTHER of the younger singers rapidly rising to eminence is that gifted contralto Helen Watts. She was born in Pembrokeshire in December 1927 and although her parents possessed no great musical ability, there was a definite background of music in her family. Her brother, to mention but one other member, was a chorister at Llandaff Cathedral and afterwards went to St. John's Cambridge as a choral scholar.

She started to learn to play the piano at the age of seven, and was deeply interested in the art throughout her childhood, but had no idea that she possessed a voice above the average. Even when she went to a boarding school at thirteen (St. Mary and St. Anne's, Abbot's Bromley, Staffordshire) and was chosen for the school choir, the idea of earning a living as a singer or taking up music as a profession generally was never seriously considered. There can be no doubt that her love of music was stimulated by the many musical activities officially encouraged at school, but when she left at seventeen she resolved to devote herself to physiotherapy.

On being informed that she would have to wait a year before starting her training, her father suggested that she might like to go to the Royal Academy of Music for a while. She chose singing as her principal subject, and within a few months was agreeably surprised to find that her voice responded extremely well to the excellent training she was receiving. This discovery, and the agreeable atmosphere of life as a music student, encouraged her to try singing as a profession. She stayed at the Academy for four years, her principal teacher being Caroline Hatchard, and later took additional lessons with Frederic Jackson, a professor of the piano at the Academy with a *flair* for choir training.

Her student days over, she was now faced with the arduous problem of establishing herself as a singer. She is not likely to forget the difficulties of those early days, when the precariousness of her existence was an ever-present anxiety. She started quite literally at the bottom of the ladder, her first appointment being as a super-numerary of the BBC Chorus, which for the uninitiated means that she augmented the Chorus when additional singers were required, deputized, and was "on call" for any odd singing jobs that came along.

Her merits were soon recognised, and this appointment brought quite a substantial number of engagements for choral work as well as a few opportunities to shine as a soloist. In 1950 she received her first BBC engagement: as a soloist in a programme for the Welsh Region in which two pianists also took part. She gave a programme of English songs and received very encouraging reports.

The BBC did not make any undue haste in promoting the career of this promising young artiste, however, and it was 1953 before she first broadcast from London. This was in a Light Programme feature called "May I Introduce...." but it led to many other engagements in due course and she soon began to receive invitations from choral societies, chiefly to act as soloist in oratorio work.

Her singing of the title rôle in a broadcast performance of Gluck's *Orpheus and Eurydice* brought her to the attention of Geraint Jones, the well-known organist and conductor, who engaged her for two Bach programmes that he was about to do for the BBC. This proved to be an important stage in her career for it was the first of many engagements in what might be described as the Third Programme class of work.

Strangely enough, she was not particularly attracted to the works of Bach as a student, but later studies revealed to her the greatness of them, and it was a profound joy to her to find how well they suited her voice. It was to sing Bach that she was engaged for her first Promenade Concert in 1955, a memorable success that was repeated in the following year.

Helen Watts also made her first recording in 1955: solo parts in *Semele* and *Sosarme* (Handel) for Oiseau-Lyre (OL 50098-100; OL 50091-3). For the same company she later made a recital recording "Songs for Courtiers and Cavaliers" with Thurston Dart (OL 50128).

She was now securely established as a soloist, and her travels were taking her further afield, providing her with the experience of singing under many distinguished conductors.

Her fine voice has a compass of two octaves (G-G) but she can go higher when required. It is a warm, full-bodied contralto, steady and well-produced, but not particularly heavy. It seems to be most adaptable, hence the fairly wide range of work she undertakes.

She enjoys the lighter work with chamber ensembles equally as much as singing in the great oratorios, and is particularly successful as a recitalist. It is always a pleasure to her to be able to make up her own programme of songs. Incidentally, she does not share the opinion of so many other prominent singers that English is a difficult and unrewarding language to sing: on the contrary, she believes that it can be very beautiful indeed when sung properly, and she demonstrates this convincingly in her recitals. She is also mindful of the importance of keeping English music alive, deploring the neglect of many of our sixteenth, seventeenth and eighteenth century composers. The majority of Purcell's music appeals strongly to her, and she feels that much of the vocal and instrumental music of William Lawes[1] is worthy of revival. She is also interested in the works of many modern English composers, notably Vaughan Williams and Herbert Howells. Nevertheless, she is often heard at her best in Brahms and Bach, the *St. Matthew Passion* being one of the works in which she has frequently distinguished herself.

Miss Watts has little use for "temperament" and rather prides herself on being a "normal" woman, enjoying sewing, cookery and other domestic arts as her chief relaxation. She is passionately fond of the rugged Pembrokeshire coast, enjoys swimming in the sea, and likes animals, especially dogs.

[1] William Lawes was born in Salisbury in 1602 and came to an untimely end fighting for the King at Chester in 1645.